Stephen W. Need was born in Nottingham and studied theology at King's College, London, where he completed a doctorate in Systematic Theology. He has taught New Testament Studies and Early Christianity in Chichester, Southampton and Jerusalem, and has published a number of articles in learned journals. He has travelled widely in Turkey and the Middle East, and is currently Dean of St George's College, Jerusalem.

TRULY DIVINE
AND TRULY HUMAN

The Story of Christ and the Seven
Ecumenical Councils

STEPHEN W. NEED

First published jointly in 2008 in Great Britain by SPCK
and in the United States by
Hendrickson Publishers, Inc.

Society for Promoting Christian Knowledge
36 Causton Street
London SW1P 4ST
www.spckpublishing.co.uk

Hendrickson Publishers, Inc.
P.O. Box 3473
Peabody
Massachusetts 01961-3473

British Library Cataloguing-in-Publication Data
A catalogue record for this book is available from the British Library

SPCK ISBN 978-0-281-05876-1
Hendrickson Publishers ISBN 978-1-59856-2996

Typeset by Graphicraft Ltd, Hong Kong
First printed in Great Britain by Ashford Colour Press
Subsequently digitally printed in Great Britain

Produced on paper from sustainable forests

For Jill

sine qua non

Contents

Illustrations

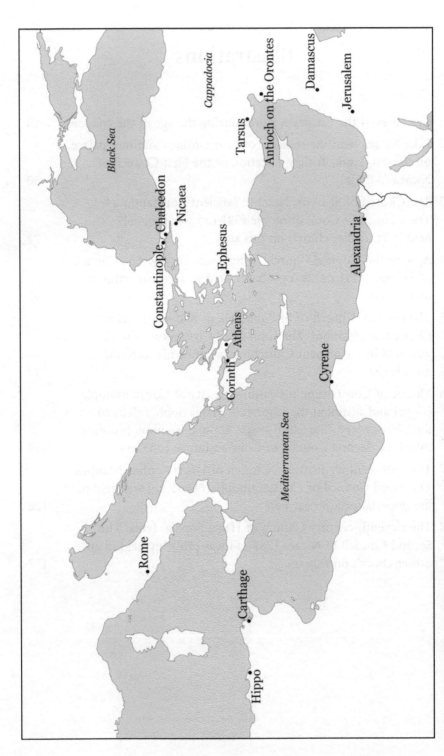

Figure 1 Key cities of the Christian world during the age of the councils

Introduction

This book is about the seven ecumenical councils of the early Church and what they had to say about Jesus Christ in the context of the developing trinitarian theology of the time. The seven councils took place between 325 and 787 in the following four cities of the Christian East: Nicaea, Constantinople, Ephesus and Chalcedon. A council was a meeting of bishops and other Christian leaders called by the emperor in order to solve theological and practical problems in the Church and to bring religious unity to the Christian world. Although there have been many different councils in the history of Christianity it is these seven that are the most important in terms of the person of Jesus Christ. Originally they were thought of as 'ecumenical' ('of the whole inhabited world') because it was hoped that representatives from the Church everywhere would be present and because the 'whole world', or much of it as then known from a Roman perspective, had become Christian under the Christian emperors from the time of Constantine. In reality, these councils were largely Eastern affairs with little or no representation from the West. The emerging concept of a 'universal church' also played a part in the idea that they were ecumenical. In addition, it is worth noting that these seven councils are regarded by many today as an important basis for ecumenical discussion and debate.

The seven councils discussed in this book arose out of the many trinitarian and christological controversies of the first eight centuries of Christianity and produced much of the language and terminology that has been used of Christ ever since. Indeed, it was these councils that established the notions of orthodoxy and heresy that are still current. These councils are crucial, therefore, to an understanding not only of Christian history but also of Christian identity today. The concern of the seven ecumenical councils was with the relations between the three persons of the Trinity and especially with the divine and human natures in Christ. It was at the Council of Chalcedon in 451, a turning point in the series, that Jesus Christ was proclaimed as 'truly divine and truly human'.

In the Orthodox churches of the East today the seven ecumenical councils are well known. Indeed, the Orthodox Church is often called the 'church of the seven councils'. Other churches acknowledge different numbers of councils. In the sixth century Pope Gregory the Great (540–604) likened the first four councils to the four New Testament Gospels in terms of their importance and authority and those four are still central to Western Christianity today. In fact, the statement produced at the Council of Chalcedon, the so-called 'Chalcedonian Definition', remains the official teaching on Christ in all the Western churches, including both the Roman Catholic Church and those churches that arose out of the Reformation in sixteenth-century Europe. The Anglican Communion accepts the first four ecumenical councils as the most important. The Roman Catholic Church accepts all seven councils but also acknowledges another 14, including the more recent Second Vatican Council of 1962–5, making a total of 21 in all. For reasons that are made clear in this book, some of the Eastern churches did not and still do not acknowledge the Council of Chalcedon and only accept the first three councils, while one accepts only the first two. Wherever contemporary Christians stand in relation to the seven councils, a clear understanding of their content and significance can only help clarify what Christians believed about Christ in the past and how that might influence Christian belief today.

The story of the councils begins with the faith of the first Christians. They had come to know God in Jesus of Nazareth and sought to find the most appropriate language in which to express and articulate their new-found faith. Much of the language they used was later to become central to the deliberations and decisions of the seven councils and was to remain in use throughout Christian history. The idea of God as a Trinity developed during the period of the councils and formed the context in which questions about Jesus were asked and answered. Trinitarian theology and Christology were intertwined as the early Christians sought the most appropriate language to use in worship and reflection.

The opening chapter of this book deals with major 'titles' of Jesus found in the New Testament, such as Lord, Christ and Son of God. The second chapter deals with the historical, geographical, philosophical and theological backgrounds to the councils and introduces readers to some of the key theologians of the period. Chapters 3 to 8 then work chronologically through the seven councils from Nicaea I (325) to Nicaea II (787), placing each one in its historical context, addressing the key doctrinal issues it dealt with, and noting other disciplinary decisions that it made. Individual theologians whose work played a part in the controversies that led up to the councils are discussed in detail. There is no discussion of the Council of Jerusalem (Acts 15), held in about 50 CE, as this was not counted in the series by the later Fathers of the Church and in any case did not deal with the triune nature of God or with the divinity and humanity of Christ. The final chapter addresses questions relating to the councils today. It considers the attitudes of the mainstream and other churches to the councils and includes a brief overview of some of the ecumenical statements that have been made by some of the churches which are still divided by the theology of the councils. Finally, an outline of some developments in modern Christology is provided, showing how serious the challenges to the councils have been since the Enlightenment.

The aim of this book is to provide introductory overviews of the theological controversies that led up to the councils, of the councils themselves, and of the decisions they made. Three main theological issues are identified throughout the book and are drawn together in the final chapter: Christology, language and salvation. It is suggested that these three elements are central to the concern of all the councils and constitute an essential part of their contribution to contemporary theology. The word 'Christology' is used by Christian theologians in a number of different ways. Its primary sense is the relation between the divinity and the humanity within the person of Christ himself. It is in this sense that the word 'Christology' is used in this book. Although all Christology throughout the period of the councils had its roots in wider trinitarian theology, the main interest of this book is in how the divinity and the humanity within the person of Christ were seen to relate to each other during the period of the councils. The concern with human language is then simply with the language used of that relation. This dimension became particularly problematic in the controversy between Cyril and Nestorius in the fifth century. Salvation has also been understood by theologians in different ways. In the East, where the councils took place, the idea of humanity 'participating' in the divine life and even becoming 'divinized' has been important. In the West, salvation has been understood more in terms of 'deliverance' from sin. In this book the Eastern sense is largely in mind although there have been different senses and emphases even there. In addition to matters concerning the Trinity, Christology, language and salvation the councils addressed a number of other matters, some of which will be noted and discussed.

Many Western Christians and others have never heard of the first seven ecumenical councils of the Church, let alone understood their meaning and significance. Others see them as purely political events. Obviously there is a limit to the detail that can be included in a book of this size, especially as its scope stretches across eight centuries. Scholars hold a wide range of different views on most of the issues dealt with and often approach the basic subject matter in fundamentally different ways. They disagree about how best to think of the different theologies of the period, and even argue over basic historical facts because of conflicting ancient sources. No attempt is made in this book to articulate all possible views and interpretations.

In general, I have decided to characterize the basic christological controversies of the period by seeing them in terms of two traditions, associated respectively with the ancient cities of Antioch and Alexandria. This characterization provides a guiding principle which will help readers with little or no knowledge of the subject to find their way through a long and confusing period of church history and to get a grasp on some of the main issues involved; it should not be taken as a definitive categorization of all the material concerned. As will be seen, there was a great deal of diversity of Christian belief in the early centuries, stretching across a wide geographical area. Furthermore, I have used words such as 'Arian', 'Monophysite' and 'Nestorian' frequently throughout the book, with broad meanings. These words are often rejected these days on the grounds that they are misleading and pejorative. But I have kept them as part of a framework designed to help readers with no background find their way through some highly complex developments. It will be helpful to bear in mind throughout that key words like these have meant different things at different times and in different places.

In the end, anyone reading this book should be able to see what the seven ecumenical councils were basically all about and why Jesus Christ gradually came to be portrayed as 'truly divine and truly human'. While most of the discussion is philosophical or theological it is also historical and geographical and I hope that readers will get a sense of the individual cities in which the councils were held through the 'Historical excursus' boxes and the photographs.

This book has arisen out of teaching Early Christianity in colleges for more than 25 years, and more recently to groups in Turkey, where the locations of some of the ancient councils can still be visited. I would like to thank my colleagues and students at Chichester Theological College (1984–90) and La Sainte Union College (1990–9) in the University of Southampton, and those at St George's College, Jerusalem (1996–), for stimulating questions and discussions. A number of individuals have been particularly helpful during the time of writing, including the Revd Dr John Binns, Dr Brad Nystrom and the Revd Canon Hugh Wybrew. I would like to thank them for their comments on various drafts of the manuscript. I would also like to thank Mr Mehmet Tanriverdi for his enthusiastic guidework at sites in Turkey related to the councils. In addition, thanks must go to Rebecca Mulhearn and various readers at SPCK who have helped enormously in getting this book into shape. Any errors, of course, are my own responsibility.

Finally, I would like to thank my wife, Jill Dampier, for her patience, support and encouragement. I will always treasure the long, peaceful hours at Pilot Hill, California where I could 'live the councils' without interruption and where most of the work was done. I dedicate the book to Jill.

Stephen W. Need
Jerusalem

1

In the beginning
The titles of Jesus

The story of Christ and the seven ecumenical councils of the Church is largely the story of how and why Jesus of Nazareth gradually became proclaimed as 'truly divine and truly human'.* It is the story of the centuries of trinitarian and christological debate that led up to this proclamation at the Council of Chalcedon in 451 and of the years of controversy and schism that followed it. The faith that was proclaimed at Chalcedon has remained central to Christianity in one way or another down the centuries since and many Christians today would claim that a belief in Christ's divinity and humanity lies at the very heart of their faith. There is no doubt that Jesus of Nazareth has always given rise to a multitude of different reactions. Already during his own ministry he was seen by some as more than an ordinary human being, making God known anew in people's lives.

The early Christians were people whose lives had been radically changed by Jesus and in the light of his life, death and resurrection they saw God, the world and their own salvation in new ways. Indeed, it was in Jesus that they believed God had offered them the possibility of a new relationship with him. Whether Jews or Gentiles, they took existing language familiar to them from their own cultures and religions and gave it new meaning as they applied it to Jesus. They used titles such as Lord, Saviour, Son of God and Son of Man as they struggled to express their new-found faith and to form their new religious identity. They used the Hebrew word 'Messiah', meaning 'anointed one', of Jesus and eventually translated it into its Greek equivalent 'Christos' or 'Christ'. After the resurrection, Christians experienced Jesus as still somehow present with them in their worship and also prayed for his return. One of the earliest Christian prayers, the Aramaic *maranatha*, 'Come Lord' (1 Cor. 16.22; cf. Rev. 22.20), indicates

---

* The expression 'truly divine and truly human' comes from the Chalcedonian Definition of faith, formulated at the Council of Chalcedon. It refers to the two natures of Christ, the divine and the human. See Chapter 6.

1

the early Christian hope that Jesus their Lord would soon be with them again but in a new way. Gradually, Jesus became thought of as so closely related to God that he was spoken of in terms often used of God himself. The Jewish tradition of 'Wisdom' and the Greek idea of the Logos were both used of Jesus in the first century and he rapidly became regarded as having been 'pre-existent' and even as having played a significant part in God's eternal purposes and creative acts. The language the early Christians used for Jesus became an important part of the theology of the councils in the following centuries, though often used in new senses. It is important, therefore, to begin a study of Christ and the seven ecumenical councils of the Church by looking at the titles of Jesus found in the New Testament.

(a) Lord, Saviour, Son of God, Son of Man and Christ

One of the most important words the first Christians used of Jesus was Lord (Rom. 1.4; 1 Cor. 1.3). This is already evident in the Aramaic *maranatha*, 'Come Lord'. Behind the English word 'Lord' lie the Hebrew *adon*, the Aramaic *mar* and the Greek *kurios*, all of which had a wide spectrum of meanings in the ancient world. In the Greek New Testament the word 'Lord' is *kurios* and could simply be a title of respect such as the English 'Sir' used by children in school. In the Hebrew Bible the letters YHWH are used to indicate the unutterable name of God and in the Greek translation of the Hebrew Bible (the Septuagint or LXX) these letters are translated by *kurios*. In the Septuagint, then, 'Lord' is effectively the name for God, more akin perhaps to 'Sir' when it is used as a term of deep reverence. The word *kurios* was also used in the pagan world to address the many gods that people worshipped.

In the New Testament, 'Lord' is used widely, has a number of different emphases, and is not used only of Jesus. It can refer to someone to whom respect is due, such as teachers and rabbis or owners of property or slaves (Matt. 21.30; Mark 12.9; Luke 12.42–47), but it can also be used of God (Matt. 5.33; 11.25; Mark 12.29–30; Acts 2.39; 4.26; Rom. 4.6–8; 11.2–4). The Apostle Paul uses 'Lord' of Jesus about 230 times, for example in 1 Thessalonians with the return of Jesus at the end of time very much in mind (4.13—5.3). In Israel's wisdom tradition, as we shall see, the Logos was seen as God's instrument of creation and Paul now connects Jesus as Lord with the whole of creation. It is through the 'Lord Jesus Christ' that all things exist (1 Cor. 8.5–6; cf. John 1.3; Heb. 1.2–3). For Paul, therefore, Jesus has a special role in God's creative activity and purposes and a cosmic significance as Lord (cf. Phil. 2.9–11). The most significant New

Testament use of 'Lord', however, comes in Luke's Gospel and the Acts of the Apostles. In the Gospel before the crucifixion, it is used of Jesus only by inspired people (1.43, 76) or an angel (2.11). But after the resurrection the disciples call Jesus Lord (24.34). In Acts, Lord is used of God and of Jesus but by now Jesus' resurrection is central to his status as Lord, and he is Lord both of believers and of the Church (Acts 1.21; 4.33; 8.16; 15.11; 16.31; 19.5, 13, 17; 20.24, 35; 21.13). In John's Gospel, Thomas says to the risen Jesus, 'My Lord and my God' (20.28), echoing an expression often used for the Roman emperor and indicating a semi-divine status: *Dominus et Deus Noster*. From all this it is easy to see that even though there were different meanings of 'Lord' it was used very early on to indicate Jesus' particularly close relation to God and was much more than simply a title of respect.

A word that was often used for Jesus by some New Testament writers alongside 'Lord' was 'Saviour'. Jesus' name, like that of Joshua in the Hebrew Bible, means 'the Lord saves' or 'the Lord is salvation', and the significance of this for early Christians was considerable. Both the Hebrew and the Greek words that lie behind 'saviour' and 'salvation' all have very broad meanings but the basic idea is one of 'helping', 'protecting', 'preserving', 'delivering' or 'liberating' and therefore of 'making safe'. There are several Hebrew words that lie behind the English 'saviour' (mostly stemming from the root *yasha*, to save or deliver; cf. *goel*, to redeem) and these have a predominantly physical sense. They are used, for example, in relation to military victory, defeat or deliverance (Judg. 8.22; 15.8; 1 Sam. 14.45; 23.5; 2 Sam. 19.3; 2 Kgs 13.7; and Ps. 91.16). They are used predominantly of God's saving activity in the events of the Exodus (Exod. 14.30) and of his saving acts at the end of time (Ezek. 34.22). The emphasis of this word is clearly on physical safety but the meaning can stretch to 'inner safety', 'personal integrity', 'well-being' and 'health'. There were other people in ancient Israel who were saviours or deliverers (Judg. 3.9, 15, 31; 2 Kgs 13.5; Neh. 9.27) but the word was used particularly of God's actions for his people (Ps. 24.5; 27.1; 35.3; Isa. 12.2; 17.10; 43.3; Jer. 14.8; Mic. 7.7).

In the Greek world the word 'saviour' (Greek *soter*) also basically meant 'helper' and could be used of a wide variety of people. It was used of the many pagan gods, such as Zeus, Heracles, Isis, Serapis and Mithras, who helped and saved their worshippers in different ways in daily life. Perhaps the most popular god of whom 'saviour' was used was Asclepius, who was specifically associated with healing and whose shrines of healing spread across the Greek and later the Roman worlds. In the healing cults the Greek saviour gods brought physical, mental and spiritual healing to their worshippers. Parallels were frequently drawn between the activities of the gods and those of rulers and others but the title did not necessarily indicate divine status. Others in Greek society could also be called 'saviour', for example philosophers such as Epicurus; rulers, statesmen and politicians such as Philip of Macedon; and doctors and physicians. Perhaps the most famous case of the use of this word in pagan literature is for the ruler Ptolemy I, whom the people of Rhodes called 'saviour' when he helped them in time of war. In the Roman world 'saviour' (Latin *salvator*) had the same meaning and was used of emperors, especially Hadrian in the second century CE, who gave help and protection to a number of cities. It should also be noted that, as in Greece, 'saviour' was used widely in Roman society and was not reserved for the emperor alone. As in Greece, it did not necessarily have connotations of 'divine'.

The Hebrew, Greek and Roman backgrounds therefore show that the word 'saviour' had a very broad series of meanings. All the meanings indicated here were eventually to find their ways into Christian concepts of salvation. In the New Testament the Greek word *soter* is in fact used quite sparingly. It occurs both with the expression 'Lord' (Luke 2.11; Phil. 3.20; 2 Pet. 1.11; 2.20; 3.2, 18) and independently of it (2 Tim. 1.10; Titus 2.13; cf. Matt. 1.21, where we see it as rooted in the meaning of Jesus' name). Although Paul does not use 'saviour' very much he certainly sees Jesus as Saviour (Phil. 3.20; Eph. 5.23) and uses the verb 'save' chiefly with reference to the future and the end of time (cf. Rom. 5.8–11 and 8.24). In the Gospels Jesus is a saviour and as people enter the Kingdom of God it is the whole person that is 'saved' (Mark 5.34; 10.52). In the Fourth Gospel Jesus is 'saviour of the world' (John 4.42; cf. 1 John 4.14). In later centuries 'saviour' was used of Gnostic leaders and salvation was associated with 'knowledge' and the escape of the spirit from the physical body.

In the New Testament 'Lord' is far more important than 'Saviour' as a title for Jesus but the early Christians clearly used both. From this, it can be seen that they respected Jesus as their helper and protector, the one who made them safe and whole, particularly with a view to their place in the new age, which they saw as imminent. They saw him as playing a particular part in God's purposes and as revealing to them what God was like. Indeed, Jesus had transformed their very understanding of God and had brought them into a new relationship with him.

The early Christians also saw Jesus as Son of God. This expression was not peculiar to Christianity and was well known in the religions of ancient Greece and Rome as well as in Judaism. It referred simply to someone who was in good standing with a god or was a god's special representative on earth. In ancient Greece, Zeus was the father of all men and all men were therefore his sons. Greek philosophers, some of the rulers of ancient Egypt, and Roman emperors were often called 'son of god'. The expression was also important in Judaism and was widely used. All men were sons of God simply because they were created by God. Male Israelites were called 'son of God' (Deut. 14.1; 32.5); the whole of Israel could be called a 'son of God' (Exod. 4.22–23; 1 Chr. 17.13; Hos. 11.1); and important individuals in Israel such as the righteous, the wise or charismatics were called 'son of God' (Wisd. 2.1–18; Sir. 4.10). In Ps. 2.7 the king has been begotten by God and is, therefore, a son of God (cf. 2 Sam. 7.14). Heavenly creatures such as angels were also called 'son of God' or 'son of the gods' (Ps. 29.1; 89.6; Dan. 3.25; cf. Luke 20.36). The plural 'sons of God' could also be used as, for example, when the 'sons of God' came down from heaven to marry the daughters of men in Gen. 6.1–4. In the ancient world generally then, 'son of god' had a very wide use and meant simply someone associated with a god and in good standing with a god, or acting as his agent, for example a king. It did not imply divine status; that development lay in the future.

The early Christians soon applied Son of God (*huios tou theou*) to Jesus and gave it particular emphases. In Paul's letters, the idea of Jesus being God's son appears quite often (e.g. Rom. 8.29, 32; Gal. 1.16; 4.4f.). There is also the notion that believers are adopted as sons as a result of Jesus being a son (Gal. 4.4–7; cf. Rom. 8.11–16). However, Paul only uses the actual expression 'Son of God' of Jesus three times (Rom. 1.4; 2 Cor. 1.19; Gal. 2.20). In these cases Jesus is Son of God by virtue of his resurrection and exaltation. The same emphasis can be found in Acts 13.33, where Ps. 2.7 is quoted. In the Gospels, Son of God is used of Jesus very frequently. In Mark, Jesus is Son of God at 1.1 but it is at his baptism (1.11) that his sonship is really established. He is recognized as Son of God by demons (3.11) and in a number of significant places throughout the Gospel (cf. 5.7; 9.7; 12.6; 13.32; 14.61). For Mark, Jesus' status as Son of God is associated above all with his death on the cross and can be seen clearly in the words of the centurion: 'Truly this man was the [or "a"] Son of God' (15.39). Matthew uses the expression in the same way as Mark but also adds different emphases, most notably in the narrative of Jesus' birth, where Jesus is Son of God at his conception (1.23; 2.15). Luke also sees Jesus' sonship as established at his conception (1.32, 35). In John's Gospel, the expression is even more important than in the other Gospels. Here, the idea that Jesus is God's Son permeates the whole narrative (1.18, 34; 3.18, 36; 11.27; 19.7; 20.31) but it is now influenced by the notion of pre-existence: Jesus is the pre-existent Son whom the Father sends into the world (17.1f.). The idea that Jesus is God's Son is also important in the epistle to the Hebrews, where it is associated with Jesus' suffering and death (2.10; 5.8f.) and his status as high priest (4.14—5.10). It is also associated with his pre-existence: he is superior to everyone else in his relation to God because he pre-exists and has a role in God's act of creating the world (1.1–3). For the Christians for whom these texts were written, the idea that Jesus was Son of God was central and was associated with his suffering, death and pre-existence. Although not a unique title for Jesus in the ancient world, then, 'Son of God' carried particular emphases when used of Jesus: it indicated his special filial relationship with God and the belief that something of the very nature of God had been revealed in him.

Another expression used for Jesus by the first Christians was Son of Man. The meaning of this expression is notoriously difficult to establish and it had different meanings at different times and in different contexts. Some of the early Fathers of the Church used Son of God to mean Jesus' divinity and Son of Man to mean his humanity but these are certainly not the original meanings; if anything they are the opposite. In the Hebrew Bible, 'son of man' (*ben adam*) occurs frequently, for example in the Psalms, where it seems to mean simply 'man' in the sense of 'humanity' (e.g. Ps. 8.4; 80.17). It also occurs in the book of Ezekiel over a hundred times and refers to the prophet himself. Once again it seems to mean simply 'man' (e.g. Ezek. 2.1, 3, 8; 3.1, 4; 4.1; 5.1). More significantly, perhaps, it occurs in the apocalyptic book of Daniel at 7.13. A heavenly vision is under way and God is seated on his throne. Then, 'one like a son of man' appears and comes to the throne. He is obviously a human being, as distinct from the animals that have already appeared, but his setting in the heavenly court indicates that he is at least a very special man. In the narrative of the book of Daniel he represents the 'saints of the most high', who are Israel. 'Son of man' also occurs in the book of Enoch and in 2 Esdras (or 4 Ezra), where the meaning is largely the same as that in Daniel 7. In the Dead Sea Scrolls the expression occurs mostly in the plural although the singular does occur, and by contrast with the use in Daniel it has very human and natural associations such as death.

In the New Testament there are some distinctive features in the use of Son of Man (*huios tou anthropou*) for Jesus. For a start, it only appears on the lips of Jesus and apart from three occurrences (Acts 7.56; Rev. 1.13; 14.14) is found entirely in the Gospels. The main difference, however, is that it now has a definite article and has become in effect a title: Jesus is *the* Son of Man. It remains something of a mystery both when and why this occurred but it is clear that for the Gospel writers it is a very significant title. In Mark, the expression 'Son of Man' carries Jesus through three key phases: first, as an earthly figure (2.10, 28); second, like 'Son of God', in relation to his suffering and death (8.31; 9.31; 10.33; 14.41); and third, more clearly associated with the figure of Dan. 7.13, as the heavenly figure that will come in the future (13.26; 14.62). In Matthew there is even more of an emphasis on his future coming (10.23; 19.28; 25.31–46) while in Luke, 'Son of Man', like 'Son of God', has become something of a general title for Jesus (6.22; 18.8; 19.10). In John, 'Son of Man' is more important than ever. It is associated once again with Dan. 7.13 and has become a mechanism by which Jesus is portrayed as a suffering and dying saviour. It occurs 13 times in the Gospel, all in the first half (1.51; 3.13, 14; 5.27; 6.27, 53, 62; 8.28; 9.35; 12.23, 34 (twice); 13.31) and carries the central theological idea of the glorification of Jesus through his death. Overall, then, 'Son of Man' was central to the early Christian sense of who Jesus was and it was especially associated with his death. It is interesting, however, that this title, although it was used by the early Fathers of the Church, was the least important in the later theology of the councils: it was chiefly used to speak of Jesus' humanity, a usage quite contrary to its main sense in the Gospels.

'Christ' or 'Messiah' is probably the best known of the titles the early Christians used of Jesus. Basically, *christos* (Christ) is the Greek translation of the Hebrew *mashiach* (messiah) and simply means 'anointed one'. However, 'messiah' occurs quite infrequently in the Hebrew Bible and there is very little expectation there of a future figure that specifically bears that name. There are certainly people in Israel's history who are anointed: kings of Israel, for example Saul (1 Sam. 9.16), David (2 Sam. 2.4–7), Absalom (2 Sam. 19.10) and Solomon (1 Kgs 1.34, 39); priests, for example Aaron (Exod. 29.7; Lev. 8.12), Zadok (1 Chr. 29.22); and prophets, namely Elisha (1 Kgs 19.16). These had been specially chosen by God for a specific purpose and therefore had a special relationship with him. Sometimes, a king of Israel is actually called the 'anointed one' or 'the Lord's anointed' (e.g. Ps. 45.6–7; 89.20; 132.10), and on one occasion Cyrus, king of Persia, is called 'anointed' (Isa. 45.1) because he is God's agent for the rescue of his people from Babylon. There are references to kings ruling a future ideal age but these are not referred to as 'messiah' (cf. Isa. 7.14; Mic. 5.2; Zech. 9.9). In the Dead Sea Scrolls, there are two messiahs: an 'anointed one of Aaron', and an 'anointed one of Israel'. But there is no single 'messianic figure' in ancient Judaism whom all Jews were expecting to appear in the future. What is clear, however, is that an 'anointed one' had a special relationship with God and a special role in God's purposes in creation and history. This obviously put the 'messiah' very close to God and his purposes.

In the New Testament, 'Christ' is used about five hundred times and the Apostle Paul uses it 270 times. Paul's use is very broad and even though he tends to use it as a second name for Jesus it is clearly more than that. He associates it especially with Jesus' death (Rom. 5.6, 8; 14.15; 1 Cor. 8.11; 2 Cor. 5.14; 1 Thess. 5.9–10), with his resurrection (Rom. 8.34; 14.9; 1 Cor. 15.3–5; 2 Cor. 5.15), with believers and their baptism (Rom. 6.3–11), and with followers of Christ (Rom. 6.11; 8.1; 12.5), and even speaks of being 'in Christ' (Gal. 3.26–28; cf. Rom. 8.10). He also links Christ with the end of the age (Phil. 1.6, 10; 2.16). In the Gospels, the word has similar associations. Mark uses 'Jesus Christ' in his opening verse (1.1) and then 'Christ' in the context of his emphasis on Jesus' suffering and death (8.29; 9.41; 12.35–37; 13.21–22; 14.61; 15.32); and Matthew has similar emphases (1.16–17, 18; 11.2; 16.16; 23.10; 24.5; 26.68; 27.17–22). Luke tends to merge 'Christ' with other expressions. He writes of the 'Lord's Christ' (2.26; cf. Acts 4.26) and uses 'Christ' with 'Son of God' (4.41; 22.67–70), although his emphases are still on Jesus' death and resurrection. In John, 'Christ' is clearly used as a title for Jesus both as the pre-existent Logos and as the earthly Jesus (1.17; 4.25; 7.26, 27, 31; 11.27; 17.3; 20.31). Other New Testament writers also use the word as a vehicle of their own individual theologies: Hebrews (3.6, 14; 9.11–28; 13.8), 1 Peter (1.18–19; 2.21; 4.13–16), the Johannine Epistles (1 John 1.3; 3.23; 5.20; 2 John 7–9) and Revelation (1.1, 2, 5; 11.15; 12.10; 20.4–6) all use the word regularly of Jesus. It is clear that the word 'Christ' is used in the New Testament more in relation to Jesus' death and resurrection than to any 'messianic' status he might have had and for the New Testament writers it was clearly in his death and resurrection that Jesus was God's 'anointed one'; it was in this respect, they maintained, that he was most closely connected to God. As with the other titles, then, the first Christians used 'Christ' of Jesus to mark his special relationship with God and his special role in God's purposes. In his life, death and resurrection Jesus had revealed God to them.

In relation to all these titles it is clear that the original senses often slipped from view fairly quickly as they started to be used for Jesus. Originally rather fluid and poetic expressions from the Hebrew and Greek traditions, they took on a more solid sense and came to mean specific things to Christians when they were used of Jesus. 'Christ', for example, seems virtually to have become part of Jesus' name quite early on and to some extent the original associations faded. The same applies to 'Son of Man'. But all these expressions continued to be used of Jesus in different ways by different writers in the early centuries and development in their use by early Christians is certainly discernible. In addition to the titles Lord, Saviour, Son of God, Son of Man and Christ, the early Christians drew upon the even more powerful notions of 'wisdom', 'word' (or *logos*) and 'pre-existence' when they spoke about Jesus. These ideas enabled them to articulate their belief that Jesus had a key role in the ultimate purposes of God in creation, history and revelation. Furthermore, when it came to the trinitarian and christological controversies of later centuries and to the councils themselves, these ideas became even more important than some of the titles already discussed: they had an element of abstraction that made them more useful in quasi-philosophical discussion of Jesus' person and role.

(b) Wisdom and Word

The idea that Christ was God's 'Wisdom' can be found already in 1 Cor. 1.24. The Hebrew word for 'wisdom' is *hokmah* and the Greek is *sophia*. The tradition of thought about God's wisdom in ancient Israel was very strong and produced literature such as the books of Job, Proverbs, Ecclesiastes, Ecclesiasticus and the Wisdom of Solomon. The 'wisdom literature', which saw God's 'wisdom' as a poetic symbol of his expression of himself in the world and in the human mind, had a profound influence upon both Israelite and early Christian theology. The book of Proverbs is probably the best place to get an idea of the Israelite 'wise saying' and Proverbs 8 certainly became central to the later trinitarian and christological controversies that led to the councils. Proverbs consists of pithy sayings that conjured up the truths of life as they were learnt in actual experience. For example, sayings concerning work and wealth (Prov. 6.6; 22.1) arose directly out of everyday life and provided a quick, simple but often profound moral guide. At the deeper level wisdom had to do with 'the ways of the world' and with 'the ways of God'. It was not only a matter of practical rules by which to live; wisdom was concerned with the eternal truths of the universe and the ultimate nature of God. In Proverbs, Wisdom is personified as a beautiful young woman who calls to the 'sons of men' to follow her (Prov. 8.1f.). In Prov. 8.22f. she exists before the creation of the world and is with God at the beginning of his work, 'the first of his acts of old'; she is God's helper in creating the world (8.27f.; cf. 3.19, 20); and is a source of life (3.18; 8.35). The image teaches that the world is made rationally by God, and a number of scholars have even claimed that wisdom was a separate dimension within the being of God, rather like the 'Word of God' in John 1.1.

For the early Christians the language of wisdom was a particularly appropriate way to speak about Christ. It personified a particular element in God's purposes; it was pre-existent (God had always been 'wise') and was God's agent in creating the universe. It might also be seen as a distinct being within God's very nature. Even more significant than simply using the word 'wisdom' was when a writer drew upon the whole wisdom tradition, as in the 'christological hymn' of Col. 1.15–20. There, Christ is 'the first-born of all creation' (v. 15); 'in him all things were created' (v. 16); and 'in him all things hold together' (v. 17). Thus, Christ steps into the shoes of Wisdom and expresses God's good creative purpose. The idea that Christ was pre-existent, had a role in creating the world, and was even a special part of God's being became extremely powerful in the early Christian imagination. However, it was precisely in relation to the question of how all this could have come about that the controversies that led to the seven ecumenical councils emerged. Texts like Prov. 8.22 could be interpreted in dramatically different ways by different people and calling Jesus the 'Wisdom of God' still left a great deal of disagreement about his ultimate relation to God. Indeed, as we shall see, it was exactly this problem that lay at the heart of the Arian controversy and of the Council of Nicaea in the fourth century.

Probably the most important word the early Christians used in relation to Jesus, and one that was to become influential in the period of the councils, is 'word' or *logos*. In many ways *logos* is parallel to 'wisdom' and is an alternative expression of God's creative rationality. *Logos* is, of course, a Greek word and a Greek concept, but behind it lay the Hebrew *dabar* and the Aramaic *memra*. The Hebrew and Aramaic words indicated the active power of God in speech. When the prophets of ancient Israel proclaimed that 'the word of the Lord' had come to them (Isa. 9.8; Jer. 1.4; Ezek. 1.3; Amos 3.1) this is the term they used. In the Genesis narrative, God 'speaks' in the process of creating the world (1.3, 6, 9) and in the Psalms God's speaking is associated with his very act of creation: 'By the word [*dabar*] of the Lord the heavens were made' (Ps. 33.6). In Jewish thinking, then, *dabar* was a metaphor for the activity of God in creation. In the Septuagint, *dabar* is translated as *logos*. The word *logos* can be closely related to 'wisdom' (Wisd. 9.1) and it is sometimes claimed that *logos* is the masculine equivalent to the feminine 'wisdom' (*sophia*). In Greek thought, *logos* not only meant 'word' but also 'discourse' and 'rationality'.

It did not only mean the spoken word, although it included that, but indicated the whole concept of order and rational meaning in the universe. Indeed, *logos*, like 'logic', indicated reason, rationality and order. Rather like 'wisdom' in the Jewish world, *logos* soon came to have a universal meaning: it was the rational principle or agent which permeated the universe at every level. It was the rational 'glue' that stuck everything together, made sense of the world and gave meaning to life. Again like 'wisdom', *logos* soon came to be thought of as an aspect of the divine life and therefore as pre-existent. It was now 'the Logos'. The great first-century Jewish scholar Philo of Alexandria, who was influenced by the Greek Platonist tradition, understood *logos* in this way and associated it with the structure of the cosmos, with wisdom and with the pre-existent Torah. For the first Christians, then, *logos* was the active speech of God in creation and in his message to the prophets, and indicated the rational ordering that upheld the universe.

In the New Testament, the word *logos* appears in the prologue to John's Gospel: 'In the beginning was the Word, and the Word was with God, and the Word was God' (1.1). Recalling Gen. 1.1, the writer claims that the 'Word' was there 'in the beginning'. The Word is not only 'with God' but *is* God. Here a very important distinction is made between the Word and God, for they are apparently distinct as well as very closely related. The Word who is with God is also the agent of creation, for 'all things were made through him' (v. 3). In the most important verse of all, the writer claims that the Logos 'became flesh': 'And the Word became flesh and dwelt among us' (v. 14). This verse is central not only to the prologue but also to all the subsequent trinitarian and christological debates and councils that will be dealt with in this book. The verse claims that the 'Logos', which Jews thought of as God's activity in creation and in speaking to the prophets of Israel, and which for Greeks was the rational principle of order in the universe, now 'became flesh' in Jesus of Nazareth. The Logos had become united with the whole human condition. The word 'became' here is notoriously difficult to interpret. It does not mean that the Logos was 'changed into' flesh and ceased to be the Logos; rather, the Logos became united with flesh in the incarnation. John 1.14 does not venture to say how or in what manner this happened, just that it did happen; nor is this an issue that the author takes up elsewhere in the Gospel. We might call it virtually a poetic statement of Jesus' role. The idea of the Logos, then, was absolutely crucial to the way that early Christians came to think of Jesus' relation to God. As we shall see, much of the trinitarian and christological debate of the period of the seven ecumenical councils was spent trying to answer two key questions that arose from John's prologue: what ultimately was the relation between God and the Logos? and how did the Logos and *sarx* or flesh (human existence) come together in Jesus of Nazareth? In fact, even though John's prologue was used widely in the later trinitarian and christological controversies it does not answer either of these questions, simply because they had not yet come to be seen as issues.

Fundamental to the titles of 'Word' and 'Wisdom' is the concept of 'pre-existence'. Though absent from the Gospels of Matthew, Mark and Luke, it is clear that this was an important concept in early Christian thinking about Jesus. There are two possible meanings of 'pre-existent' in this context: first, 'existing before the birth of Jesus': this is the idea that the Logos, for example, simply existed before Jesus' birth; second (incorporating the first), 'existing before creation and from eternity'. It is this second meaning that is most important here. The key point is this: ancient Jews and Christians all believed that God was the creator of the universe. As the creed produced at Nicaea was later to say, they believed that he had created everything, both 'visible and invisible'. Not only was God seen as creator of the two dimensions of reality that people experienced, however, he was ultimate in the sense that before he created anything at all there was just God. For people who thought in this way, the period of 'pre-existence' was the period before God began to create the world or before he became involved in and with the world. Most theologians in the ancient world believed that when God created the world he also created time. It is, of course, notoriously difficult to talk about 'a time before time' because the language of time is inappropriate for that period. However, there was and is no other language to use of God than time-bound human language. Expressions such as 'a time outside time', 'a time before time', 'eternal' and 'eternality', therefore, inevitably arose in these debates. The expression 'pre-existence', then, refers simply to the 'time' before God began to create the world and act within it.

As the early Christians began to think about the ultimate significance of Jesus and as they associated him with God ever more closely, they used 'wisdom' and 'word' language to link him up with the eternal being of God. There was a 'time before time' when there was only God and they wanted Jesus to be associated with God in that. Apart from appearing in the wisdom literature and the prologue to John's Gospel, the idea of 'pre-existence' in this second sense can be found in Paul's letter to the Philippians and in the epistle to the Hebrews. In Philippians, Paul writes, 'Have this mind among yourselves, which you have in Christ Jesus, who, though he was in the form of God, did not count equality with God a thing to be grasped, but emptied himself, taking the form of a servant' (2.5–7). The passage goes on to speak of Christ's humility and death on a cross and of his 'super-exaltation' as Lord of the universe. But the opening words of the passage claim that Jesus was 'in the form of God'. Although these words can be interpreted in different ways, they are usually taken to refer to the pre-existent life that Christ had with God before the incarnation and by implication before creation (cf. 1 Cor. 8.6). Taking a related yet distinct line in the opening verses of the epistle to the Hebrews, the writer claims that Christ is God's agent of creation, 'through whom also he created the world' (1.2). He is also 'upholding the universe by his word of power' and 'reflects the glory of God and bears the very stamp of his nature' (1.3). It is possible that Hebrews was written to refute the idea that Jesus was just an angel. In the theology of the Judaism of the time angels were very popular and Hebrews could have been written to stress that Jesus was more than an angel: he was the pre-existent Son. This idea of pre-existence, then, soon became very powerful in Christian thinking about Jesus and enabled the first Christians to associate him very closely with God and his ultimate purposes in creation and history. Indeed, this concept was to remain central to the trinitarian and christological controversies and to the seven major councils. Above all, it had the capacity to take the discussion into a much more philosophical and intellectually ambitious sphere.

The final question here, and in some ways the most important, is this: did the early Christians actually think of Jesus as God? Did they already think of him as 'truly divine and truly human'? In his life, death and resurrection and in his miracles or 'works of mighty power' they saw him doing the work of God and it is clear that from the earliest days they thought of him as revealing God to them. They then spoke of him in language that associated him very closely with God and used concepts such as wisdom, Logos and pre-existence, which placed him in the realm of the divine in a very specific way. But did the early Christians actually think of Jesus as God? Did they identify him with God? This is a question that has occupied commentators for centuries and still provokes very diverse answers today. We have seen that the titles the early Christians used of Jesus had a wide range of meanings and were used of a wide range of people. The Emperor Augustus, for example, was called Son of God, Lord, and Saviour. It is important to remember this when trying to assess what the first Christians meant by the language they used of Jesus. Even though they clearly thought of him as one whose life was bound up with God's life and thought of him as doing the work of God, achieving the purposes of

God and revealing God to them, and even though they used language that associated him very closely with God, it is less clear that in the early stages they thought of him in exactly the sense that the later councils were to think of him, that is as 'God incarnate'. Indeed their Jewish background and even their wider intellectual formation did not generally allow them to think in such a way. There are places in the New Testament where either the Logos or Jesus seem to be called God (John 1.1, 18; 20.28; Rom. 9.5; Phil. 2.6; Col. 1.15) but these can all be interpreted in a number of different ways and do not really amount to the philosophical claims made by the later councils. Thus, the New Testament evidence indicates that while first-century Christians thought of Jesus as Lord, Saviour, Son of God, Son of Man and Christ, and also used concepts such as wisdom, word and pre-existence to show that they thought of him as revealing God to them and as operating in very close association with God and his purposes in creation and history, they did not yet think of him specifically as having 'two natures', divine and human, as the Council of Chalcedon was to do in 451. In New Testament times, the 'high' language had perhaps better be put in the category of poetry rather than philosophy or history.

(c) Conclusion

The first Christians were people whose lives had been radically changed through their experience of Jesus. In his life, death and resurrection they had come to see something fundamentally new about God and their relationship with him. In him the nature of God had been revealed to them and through him they experienced a new sense of salvation. There were many different ideas of salvation at the time stemming from Judaism and the Graeco-Roman world, and the early Christians took up several of these and used them in their theology. They believed that Jesus had brought them substantially closer to God and made their lives complete and whole. Indeed, Jesus was now their Lord and Saviour and everything looked very different in the light of their new-found faith. The first Christians did not yet speak of Jesus as 'truly divine and truly human' but they drew on specific language from their own religious backgrounds in the Jewish, Greek and Roman worlds to articulate their understanding of Jesus' relationship with God. As this language was taken up and used specifically of Jesus it received new and varied layers of meaning. Words and expressions such as Lord, Saviour, Son of God, Son of Man and Christ were used of Jesus and became commonplace in early Christianity.

Much of this language continued to be used widely by individual theologians in later debates and in the documents of the councils. For example, Athanasius and others use the language of sonship very frequently; the creed produced at Nicaea in 325 calls Jesus Lord, Christ and Son of God; and the Chalcedonian Definition calls him Lord, Christ and Son. Equally important were the wider concepts of wisdom, word and pre-existence. These became fundamental and carried with them powerful theological associations reflecting the belief that Jesus was not only closely associated with God but actually had a special role in his ultimate purposes from before creation. Jesus was now fundamentally related to the eternal being of God; he had been there with God from the beginning, not only of time and creation, but possibly always; and he reflected the eternal glory and life of God when he became known on earth as Jesus of Nazareth. Indeed, he was a revelation of God. The three concepts of wisdom, word and pre-existence subsequently became central to the different theologies of the period. Indeed, they provided the very framework in which words such as Lord, Saviour, Son of God, Son of Man and Christ were later understood. All these titles continued to develop and some of them became particularly important to the later theology of the councils. We might say that the mainly Jewish terms in early Christianity gradually came to be seen in a different, more Greek and partly abstract light. Broadly speaking, the words 'Logos' and 'Son' became the predominant expressions for the second person of the Trinity in later centuries and these words will henceforth be used interchangeably when referring to Jesus' divinity.

Even though the early Christians had found appropriate language to use of Jesus' relationship with God, many questions were yet to arise concerning exactly how the Logos or Son was ultimately related to the Father and exactly how the Logos or Son became united with the flesh of Jesus of Nazareth in the incarnation. There were many different interpretations of biblical texts, and many philosophical questions and distinctions were yet to emerge. But emerge they did, in due course, and although there were also more practical matters to be considered, the main concern of Christian theologians throughout the next seven centuries was to continue to find appropriate language for God, Jesus and salvation in the many different situations in which they found themselves. This concern provided the stuff of the trinitarian and christological controversies that gave rise to the seven ecumenical councils. Before turning to the councils themselves, however, we must consider their wider historical, theological, philosophical and geographical backgrounds.

2

A tale of two cities
Antioch and Alexandria

As the early Christians sought to express their experience of Jesus in the language available to them they drew upon a variety of words and expressions. The main ones, as we have seen, were Lord, Saviour, Son of God, Son of Man and Christ. In fact, 'Christ' was so central that even by the time of Paul it had already become something of a proper name for Jesus (Rom. 1.1; 1 Cor. 1.1). In previous Jewish usage it indicated that the person of whom it was used had a very close relationship with God and his purposes. In the early days, as Christians sought to capture the idea that Jesus was indeed God's anointed agent on earth, the word 'Christ' presented itself as especially appropriate. It had particular associations with the hopes of Israel, a factor that obviously helped bring it to the centre of early Christian thinking about Jesus. In the later debates of the councils Jesus is called Christ or Jesus Christ and for this reason we shall now mostly refer to him as Christ. But concepts such as 'Wisdom', 'Word' and 'pre-existence' became increasingly important and later determined the very mindset in which trinitarian and christological thinking was carried out. It could have been the decline of hopes linked specifically to Israel and the Jews, especially in the formulation of theological arguments, that eventually enabled 'Word', 'Son' and 'Wisdom' to become more central than 'Christ'. In any case, although most of the titles and expressions discussed in the previous chapter continued to be used widely throughout the next centuries, it was 'Wisdom', 'Word', 'Son' and 'pre-existence' in particular that became central to the debates surrounding the seven ecumenical councils. Jesus was not only Lord, Saviour and Christ, he was now predominantly the 'Wisdom of God' and the 'pre-existent Word' or 'Son'.

As the years of the first century passed and Christian communities sprang up around the Mediterranean world, radically different interpretations of Christ emerged and there were many different understandings of his relation to God, even though the language discussed in Chapter 1 was used very widely. Some, like the Ebionites, held that Jesus was merely human;

at most he was on a par with the prophets of ancient Israel. For others, like the many different and sometimes conflicting Gnostic groups, he was more of a divine figure, a mediator between God and humanity who was barely human at all. Different approaches developed in different places and key cities in the Christian world became associated with characteristic emphases. Antioch and Alexandria became particularly important. The philosophical mindset that dominated the early Christian period stemmed from Plato, although some theologians took an approach that was closer in some respects at least to Aristotle. Today, scholars even speak of 'Christianities' instead of 'Christianity' when referring to the many different theological styles and emphases of this period.

In this chapter the two theological traditions usually associated with Antioch and Alexandria will be explored, noting some key Christian thinkers of the period. The basic philosophical climate within which early Christian theologians operated will then be discussed. Different attitudes to Scripture during this period will be acknowledged and the work of two representative thinkers, Theodore of Mopsuestia and Origen, will be outlined. Finally, some comments about the importance of salvation during the period of the councils will be made. All this will set the stage for an examination in later chapters of the trinitarian and christological debates that led to the seven ecumenical councils themselves and to the idea that Jesus Christ was 'truly divine and truly human'.

(a) Antioch and Alexandria

As the early Christians refined their language about Christ and as philosophical distinctions concerning his precise relation to God were sharpened, a variety of Christian traditions grew up in different parts of the Roman Empire. In order to get a full sense of the significance of the debates that led to the councils and their claims about Christ it is important to know something of the historical settings in which the controversies took place. The whole drama of the councils was played out in six key cities around the Mediterranean: Jerusalem, Rome, Antioch, Alexandria, Ephesus and Constantinople. Five of the cities had strong associations with the apostles and this gave them a certain authority in the period with which we are concerned. The sixth, Constantinople, only gradually gained such status. The story begins, of course, in the Jewish city of Jerusalem. Jesus' death and resurrection had occurred in Jerusalem and all the apostles had been there. Christianity was soon taken to the largely Gentile city of Rome and the Apostles Peter and Paul then became associated with the capital city of the empire. They had already both been to Antioch in Syria, where the followers of Jesus were first called 'Christians' (Acts 11.26). Later tradition claimed that Mark took Christianity to Alexandria in Egypt, while Ephesus, the capital of Asia Minor, was associated with Paul and later with John and the Virgin Mary. In the fourth century, Constantine founded Constantinople as the capital of the new Christian empire. Although not originally a city with 'apostolic status', it gradually became associated with the Virgin Mary and Andrew.

Of these six cities, the most important two for our purposes are Antioch and Alexandria. An appreciation of the significance of these cities in the early Christian period and of some of the theologians associated with them will help provide the wider background to the councils. Of course, the many different strands in the development of early Christian thinking about Christ cannot be reduced to two cities, approaches or traditions. But the general designation 'Antiochene' and 'Alexandrian' has become well known and helps identify particular theological emphases, especially before the Council of Chalcedon. These designations will be used frequently in this book as shorthand for certain approaches and tendencies explained in this chapter.

Ancient Antioch is usually known as 'Syrian Antioch' or 'Antioch on the Orontes'. In the early Christian period it produced a number of key leaders and theologians who were to give 'Antiochene Christology' its characteristic features. Already in the Acts of the Apostles Antioch is important. It was probably the headquarters for Paul's several missionary journeys. The famous conflict between Peter and Paul in Paul's letter to the Galatians (ch. 2) is located there. It is also at least possible that a number of New Testament texts were written in Syria if not in Antioch itself. From the second century Antioch became even more important. Ignatius of Antioch (*c.* 35–*c.* 107 CE) wrote six surviving letters to churches in western Asia Minor and one to Polycarp in Smyrna. He visited Polycarp when he was on his way to Rome, where he was martyred in 107. Theophilus, Bishop of Antioch in the second half of the second century, was probably the first to use the word 'triad' of God in the early stages of the development of trinitarian theology. Paul of Samosata, one of the best known of the Antiochenes, was Bishop of Antioch (260–72) and seems to have taught a version of 'Monarchianism', which emphasized the unity of God rather than the distinctions within the Trinity. He probably taught that the Logos was simply an aspect of God rather than a distinct part and that it came to rest on Jesus at his baptism. The idea that Jesus was an ordinary man who was adopted by God for particular purposes later became known as 'Dynamic Monarchianism' or 'Adoptionism'. In his understanding of the Logos, Paul was probably not far from much Old Testament and New Testament usage, for in Paul's thinking the 'word' is an image for God's activity. There was also Lucian of Antioch, who was martyred for his faith *c.* 312. Like Arius, he apparently taught that the Logos was subordinate to the Father. The emphases of these theologians on the unity of God and the humanity of Jesus became dominant in later Antiochene theology and characterized the Antiochene contributions to the several councils.

Antioch became even more significant in the fourth century in terms of theologians who shaped the debates about the Trinity and Christology. John Chrysostom (*c.* 347–407) was born there and studied under Diodore of Tarsus (d. *c.* 390). John was for a while a monk in the hills of Mount Silpius near Antioch but was later ordained and became well known as a preacher in the wider area. His powerful and eloquent preaching led to his nickname 'golden mouth' or 'Chrysostom'. In his interpretation of Scripture he stressed the more straightforward meaning of the texts and was against the type of allegorization that was developing in Alexandria. John later became Bishop of Constantinople, the city that was to be the seat of Antiochene theology in the fourth and fifth centuries and where several of the councils were eventually to be held. He caused riots in the city by preaching against wealth and the excessive lifestyle of the inhabitants. John was at school with another major Antiochene theologian, Theodore of Mopsuestia (*c.* 350–428), who was eventually condemned in the so-called 'Three Chapters Controversy' at the Second Council of Constantinople in 680–1. As noted above, we shall consider Theodore's theology later in this chapter. Nestorius (b. after 351, d. after 451), another key Antiochene in the tradition of Theodore, was later Archbishop of Constantinople and provoked a major christological crisis concerning the two natures in Christ. He was eventually condemned at the Council of Ephesus in 431. We shall consider his theology in Chapter 5. Finally, Simeon the Stylite (*c.* 390–459) was best known for living on top of a pillar (*stylos*) in the area of Antioch. Simeon's type of monastic existence became popular in Syria in the fourth and fifth centuries and he himself became very famous around the Mediterranean world. A monastery grew up around his pillar and people travelled from afar to visit him. The ruins of his monastery can still be visited today near Antakya. His movement indicates the monastic context in which Christian theology during this period was often carried out. Again, typical Antiochene theological principles can be found in the writings of these theologians: the unity of

God; the humanity of Jesus; the distinction between the two natures of Christ; and the 'plain-sense' rather than the allegorical interpretation of Scripture.

Religious, cultural and linguistic issues also influenced the Antiochene tradition. It is well known that before and during the Christian period Antioch had a significant Jewish presence. Geographically the city was not far from Jerusalem. There is also evidence of a synagogue in nearby Daphne. The key evidence, however, comes from three sources: Josephus (*c.* 37–*c.* 100); the Talmud (fifth century); and the writings of John Moschus (*c.* 550–619 or 634). The size of the Jewish population in Antioch is unclear but it is obvious that Jewish theology and exegesis of biblical texts influenced Christian biblical exegesis (see the Gospel of Matthew as a possible example of such activity). Furthermore, the Jewish presence in Antioch is significant in terms of later Christian theology: the emphasis there was always on this-worldly and human rather than other-worldly and divine aspects. Indeed, it was this Semitic influence along with a possible sensitivity to Aristotelian philosophical ideals that gave Antiochene Christian theology its specific flavour. There is also no doubt that the distinctive Syriac language and culture contributed a great deal to the Antiochene tradition. The Syriac language is a version of Aramaic, the language spoken by Jesus. Versions of the Bible in Syriac and early Christian literature in Syriac, such as the poetry of Ephraim the Syrian (*c.* 306–373), influenced the Antiochene approach to theology. Tatian's *Diatessaron*, a harmony of the Gospels possibly written in the mid-second century, may also have been written in Syriac and circulated widely in the churches of the day.

Already in the first few centuries, then, the key characteristics of the Antiochene approach to Christ had been laid down. There were, of course, many different approaches to the divinity and humanity of Christ, and many different emphases even within the Antiochene tradition. But there were some characteristics that were emerging clearly: tendencies to approach things from a 'human' angle; to emphasize the unity of God; to see the Logos as subordinate to the Father; to distinguish and even separate the human from the divine; and to treat biblical texts in a straightforward rather than allegorizing manner. The Antiochene emphasis on rhetoric more than philosophy is also important here; the emphasis was on the straightforward meaning of language rather than on philosophical speculation. These tendencies were to grow and develop over the centuries of the seven councils and were to become more and more deeply rooted in the Antiochene mind.

21

Historical excursus 1: Antioch

Antioch in Syria or Antioch on the Orontes (modern Antakya in Turkey) was one of the most important cities of early Christianity. There were many cities called Antioch in the ancient world. This one became the most famous, not least because of the visit of Anthony and Cleopatra in *c.* 37 BCE. The history of the city goes back to the fourth century bce. The area where it is located may have been occupied by Greek settlers at that time but the city of Antioch itself was founded in 300 BCE by Seleucus I Nicator, one of the generals of Philip II of Macedon, who inherited the Syrian part of the empire of Philip's son, Alexander. The area was attractive for a number of reasons: it was fertile and the many springs of the area provided a plentiful supply of water; it stood on the east–west trade route dominated by silk; and it was politically strategic.

The city itself lay at the foot of Mount Silpius and on the banks of the River Orontes. Not far away, the port town of Selucea Pieria brought cargo up from the Mediterranean Sea and the nearby town of Daphne was well known for its high standard of living. In fact, Seleucus I originally created Seleucea Pieria as the capital of the Seleucid kingdom and named it after himself. Antioch was named

---

The Antiochene approach to Christ was later to become focused on Constantinople but before taking the story further we must turn to Alexandria, where different tendencies and philosophical interests were developing.

In Alexandria, a rich but very different tradition of theological thinking was also gradually emerging. Early Christian associations with the city remain obscure but the later tradition that Mark took the gospel to Alexandria eventually gave it a certain prestige. In the second century, various Gnostic groups were centred there, such as the one associated with Basilides. These varied groups usually stressed the superiority of the world of the intellect and of hidden or 'esoteric' knowledge (*gnosis*). They saw the created world of matter as inferior and sometimes as evil. The theological systems associated with these groups were characterized by numerous intermediary figures that linked the world of matter to the world of the spirit. They saw salvation as a thoroughly other-worldly or heavenly affair, stressing the importance of the spiritual and intellectual aspects of human beings over

after Seleucus' father, Antiochus. After Seleucus' death, his son Antiochus I chose Antioch as his capital. During the next two centuries it grew in power, significance and size. In the first century bce, however, a number of wars brought the city to its knees and in 83 BCE it was taken by the Armenians under Tigranes I. However, in 64 bce it was taken from him by the Romans under Pompey and made the capital of the Roman province of Syria.

Under Rome, Antioch became a buffer zone against the East and was again to grow in size and significance. Eventually, it became the third largest Roman city after Rome and Alexandria and estimates of its population have ranged between 200,000 and 500,000. It was gradually to become a centre of learning and culture and regularly hosted the Olympic Games. A number of Roman emperors embellished and glorified it, including Julius Caesar. Herod the Great donated money which enabled the main street in the city to be colonnaded, one of the famous features of Antioch in that period. Followers of Jesus were first called 'Christians' in Antioch (Acts 11.26) and in the following centuries it rapidly became one of the most significant cities for Christians.

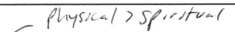

Physical > spiritual

the physical. Although Gnostics differed in many of their beliefs, their ultimate hope was that the human soul would return to the spiritual world and leave the physical completely behind. This tendency among the different Gnostic groups always to stress the spiritual and intellectual over the material or physical would influence the Alexandrian approach to Christ right through the centuries of the councils.

From the second century onwards there existed in Alexandria the so-called 'catechetical school' and quite a few of the key Alexandrian theologians were associated with it. It is unclear how formal it was but there were particular individuals at its head. The first of these was either Athenagoras or Pantaenus (d. *c.* 190) in the second century. Clement of Alexandria (*c.* 150–*c.* 215), Pantaenus' pupil, who wrote a number of books that still survive, then took over. Clement saw the Logos as central to understanding the true significance of Christianity. He was followed by Origen (*c.* 185–*c.* 254), one of the greatest of all the Alexandrian theologians, to whom we shall turn in detail later in this chapter. Dionysius the Great

Historical excursus 2: Alexandria

Alexandria is situated on the Egyptian coast (north of Cairo in Egypt), with the Mediterranean Sea to the north and Lake Mareotis to the south. It was founded by Alexander the Great in 331 BCE and had an ethnically mixed population from the beginning. It was eventually to become home to the largest Jewish community in the world outside Palestine. Unlike the Jewish community in Antioch, however, Alexandrian Judaism was thoroughly Hellenized. In the second century BCE the city came under the rule of Ptolemy I Soter and became the capital of Egypt during his reign and eventually the intellectual and cultural capital of the entire Hellenistic world. It was taken by the Romans in 30 BCE.

Like Ephesus, Alexandria was a city on the sea with a harbour that gave it cultural and political connections to the rest of the Mediterranean world. Not a lot is known about ancient Alexandria apart from the account left by the geographer Strabo. In his *Geography* he describes some aspects of the city during the time he lived there in the first century BCE. Lack of systematic archaeological excavation in the city until recently meant that very little of the city's past was known. In fact, the most significant part of ancient Alexandria is hidden under the sea due to a change in the coastline. Some recent underwater excavations, however, have given us a fuller sense of what the city was like physically. It was laid out on a 'Hippodamian grid' with streets at right angles to each other; its architect was Dinocrates of Rhodes.

The city of Alexandria was famous in the ancient world for a number of things:

1 the lighthouse, which was known as one of the seven wonders of the ancient world.

(d. *c.* 264), a pupil of Origen, was also head of the school and was active in a number of controversies in the third century. In the fourth century, Didymus the Blind (*c.* 313–398) led the school and numbered Jerome among his pupils. However, as we shall see, ideas associated with him were condemned as Origenist at the Council of Constantinople in 553.

There were also many other important theologians in Alexandria who must be noted here: Arius (*c.* 260–336), whose theology provoked

2 the famous library, housing more than a million volumes, established by Ptolemy in 306 BCE and later re-established in memory
of Alexander the Great. A symbol of great learning, the library was
comparable only with those at Pergamum and Ephesus. Its destruction is well known: it was burnt in three stages, during fires
in the first century bce and the fourth century ce, and then when
the Arabs destroyed the city in 641–2 CE.

3 the translation of the Hebrew Bible into Greek in the second
century BCE. The story is found in the *Letter of Aristeas* and tells
of 70 translators emerging independently with identical translations. This translation became known as the 'translation of the
seventy' (LXX) or the 'Septuagint'. However it came about, the
translation was a major cultural and linguistic event and Alexandria soon became the home of Hellenistic Judaism, typified by
the combination of Greek philosophy and Jewish biblical texts.

4 Philo Judaeus (*c.* 20 BCE–*c.* 50 CE), one of the greatest of Alexandria's sons, the father of Hellenistic Jewish biblical exegesis, who
lived in Alexandria at the time of Jesus of Nazareth. Philo was
the leading Hellenistic Jew of his day and wrote a number of books
on the Torah, including exegetical commentaries. Most interesting from the point of view of the councils of the Church is Philo's
teaching on the Logos, derived from the use of the idea in the
Jewish scriptures and from Greek philosophy: he saw it as central to God's purposes in the universe. Although Philo had no sys-
tematically worked-out notion of the Logos, it was an important
part of his theology and some have thought that his ideas about
it influenced Christianity.

the Council of Nicaea in 325 and gave rise to 'Arianism'; Athanasius of
Alexandria (*c.* 296–373), whose theology eventually triumphed over Arianism; Alexander, Bishop of Alexandria (d. 328), who was Athanasius'
bishop; Cyril of Alexandria (d. 444), who led the see of Alexandria against
Nestorius in the fifth century; Dioscorus (d. 454), who led the Alexandrian
reaction to the Christology that came out of the Council of Chalcedon
in 451; Eutyches (*c.* 378–454), who although he lived in Constantinople

was an extreme Alexandrian in terms of his thinking about Christ; and Severus (*c.* 465–538), a Monophysite, who was actually Patriarch of Antioch and whom we shall consider in detail in Chapter 7. All these figures contributed in their different ways to one of the most powerful traditions of theology in the ancient Church. As in the case of Antioch, there were many different approaches to the divinity and humanity of Christ in the Alexandrian tradition, and many different emphases and locations of debate. But, once again, some characteristics were emerging clearly: the Alexandrian interest was in philosophy rather than rhetoric; it was otherworldly rather than this-worldly; it tended to concentrate on the divinity of Christ and to speak of the incarnation in terms of the unity rather than the distinctions between the divinity and the humanity; it was thoroughly Platonist in its philosophical outlook, emphasizing the divinity of the Logos or Son; and it developed an allegorical method of interpreting Scripture.

The two traditions associated with Antioch and Alexandria dominated the early centuries of Christianity. Although the two schools were ultimately concerned with the same questions in theology, namely 'How was the Word related to God?', 'How were the divinity and humanity related in Christ?' and 'How was human salvation brought about in Christ?', they ended up with radically different emphases resulting largely from their different theological and philosophical approaches.

(b) The philosophical background

In the Vatican Museum in Rome a painting by Raphael entitled *The School of Athens* depicts the two great founding fathers of Western philosophy, Plato (427–347 BCE) and Aristotle (384–322 BCE), walking in the famous Academy founded by Plato in Athens. Plato extends a hand to the skies, indicating his interest in the world beyond, and carries a copy of his *Republic*, one of the dialogues in which his famous notion of 'Forms' appears. Aristotle, by contrast, extends a hand in the direction of the floor in front of them, indicating his interest in the world of matter and of everyday affairs. Under his arm, he carries a copy of his *Ethics*. The two philosophers stand at the beginning of Western philosophy like two giants whose ideas form the basis of all later philosophy and a great deal of theology too. Aristotle was Plato's pupil but there are significant differences between them. In order to understand the theology of the seven ecumenical councils and their claims about Christ it is first necessary to understand something of the philosophy of these two great men.

A useful way of approaching Plato's understanding of the world is through his so-called 'doctrine of Forms' or 'Ideas'. This is found especially in his *Meno, Phaedo* and *Republic*. Plato divides the world into two realms: that of the changing, corruptible realm of the senses, and the changeless, immaterial, eternal realm of the 'Forms'. In short, things in this world are merely shadows of their ultimate Forms or Ideas which exist in the other world. Objects in the physical world 'participate' in the ideal world of the Forms and are merely shadows of what is eternal. The Forms are not located in space or time but transcend the world of the senses. Plato uses three famous analogies to illustrate this: the sun, the line and the cave. Just as the sun gives life and growth to things on earth, so the Forms give life to the shadows in matter of which they are the Forms. A line may be divided into sections; the worlds on different sides of the line of division indicate the worlds of sense and of intellect. And finally, a group of people are bound in a cave facing away from the opening where sunlight comes in. They see shadows on the wall in front of them but cannot turn round to look outside the cave to see the world of reality indicated by the light. The shadows symbolize the world of matter that we always see; the sunlight outside indicates the world of the Forms. In all this, the world that is known from the senses, the physical world, is mere shadow while the world known through the intellect is reality. There is 'this world' and there is 'the other world'.

Over the centuries following Plato's death, his philosophy was gradually reinterpreted for new generations. Two important schools of Platonism eventually emerged: Middle Platonism and Neo-Platonism. Middle Platonism lasted roughly from 80 BCE until 220 CE. Neo-Platonism is then generally reckoned to have arisen in the person of Ammonius Saccas (*c.* 175–242), possibly a teacher of Origen and also of Plotinus (*c.* 205–270). Plotinus and his pupil Porphyry (*c.* 232–*c.* 303) were the key exponents of Neo-Platonism in its early period but it also flourished under Iamblichus (*c.* 250–*c.* 330) and Proclus (*c.* 412–485). Its basic thinking radicalized Plato's own philosophy and sharpened some of its contours. In particular, the dualism in Platonism between matter or creation and the senses on the one hand, and the intellect or reason on the other, was deepened. Indeed, matter gradually came to be seen as more and more inferior and sometimes even as evil. There were differences between Platonism and Neo-Platonism, however, even in the basic dualism. Neo-Platonism envisaged a 'great chain of being' connecting the two poles of reality. For Plotinus there was ultimately 'the One' that held all things together, then the world of the intellect, and then the world-soul which connected up with matter at the lower end of the chain, itself graded by its levels of complexity. All levels of being were connected in a graded series of realities. Plotinus' 'trinity' to some extent paralleled that in Christianity and somehow gave his system a more religious feel than Plato's had ever had. This tradition of Neo-Platonism became decidedly anti-Christian but although it continued in many different forms for many centuries, it is generally reckoned to have come to an end in the ancient world either with the closure of the Academy in Athens in 529 or when Alexandria was taken by the Arabs in 642. In the early centuries of Christianity it was Middle Platonism that was most influential but in general we shall simply use the term 'Platonism' to refer to the basic dualism and other-worldliness (already found in Plato's own writings) that characterized so much of the climate in which early Christian theology grew up.

Aristotle was a pupil of Plato in Athens. He was born in Stagira in Northern Greece and is often known as the Stagirite. Although he studied with Plato for twenty years he came to disagree with him on some important points, most notably over Plato's notion of Forms. Unlike Plato, who thought that sense-experience yielded only 'opinion' and not true knowledge, Aristotle believed that all our knowledge ultimately began with the senses. Aristotle was therefore what philosophers call an 'empiricist'. The empirical world is the world of matter, which is known through the senses. Aristotle collected facts about numerous aspects of the world and in many different subjects. His writings cover an enormous range of subjects from the human body to language, mathematics, astronomy, ethics and metaphysics. After collecting his basic facts, Aristotle tried to explain them. He saw things in terms of 'substance' and made a famous distinction between 'primary' and 'secondary' substances. He maintained that primary substances are individual objects in the world, for example individual people, animals and plants. The focus was on the solid individual thing. Secondary substances, he claimed, consist of features which are universal. Aristotle's distinction between primary and secondary substances is basically the same as that between particulars and universals. For Aristotle, unlike Plato, the individual object comes before the universal and there are no universal aspects or secondary substances without a primary subject for them to exist in. This is the fundamental dividing line between Plato and Aristotle, which was to influence later Christian theological thought: for Plato, the 'real world' was the 'other world', whereas for Aristotle, the 'real world' was 'this world'.

Plato's philosophy provided the framework in which early Christian theology grew and developed. Aristotle's philosophy was not to become really influential until the later Middle Ages, especially in the theology of Thomas Aquinas (*c.* 1225–1274). In the early centuries the study of Aristotle's philosophy was a much more elite process carried out only by experts, whereas Plato's philosophy was studied much more widely, including in Antioch. Despite the differences, however, the two approaches must not be polarized; there were early Christians who approached matters from a much more 'this-worldly' angle even within the overall Platonist mindset of the time. In spite of the early Christians' use of Platonist concepts and categories, their main claim that the Logos had become flesh (John 1.14; the 'other world' had entered 'this world') was in fact radically non-Platonist. Plato's Forms, by definition, could never enter the world of shadows. As we look at representative thinkers from the two traditions of Antioch and Alexandria and as we approach the councils themselves we shall begin to see how important the different philosophical emphases became. The tension between 'this world' and the 'other world' was ever present and the question of how the two worlds relate to each other was always there. And there were other philosophical problems and distinctions that arose in the debates surrounding the councils themselves that will be discussed in later chapters as they arise.

(c) Biblical interpretation

Several references have been made in this chapter to the interpretation of Scripture in early Christianity. There was no 'Bible' as such in the earliest days, only authoritative texts. Before Constantine, the New Testament canon or authoritative collection of texts emerged only gradually. Christians possessed the texts of the Old and New Testaments but not, as it were, in a single volume. They drew naturally on the methods of interpretation already known to them from their Jewish and Greek backgrounds. Various elements of interpretation were known in Judaism at the time, including *haggadah* (the basic story or narrative); *halakhah* (the interpretation of the story for daily life); *midrash* (a 'seeking' or 'investigation' into the text); and *pesher* (a 'solution' or 'explanation' of the text). These can be seen, for example, in the Dead Sea Scrolls. Different styles of interpretation were also known in the Greek world, especially from commentaries on the works of Plato, Aristotle, Homer and Hesiod. In both Jewish and Greek traditions the plain or literal sense of the text was important but there was also a great deal of interest in figurative language, including metaphor, symbolism, typology and allegory. In the first century all this came together most famously in the exegetical method of a Hellenistic

Jew, Philo of Alexandria. The early Christian interpretation of Scripture was also inevitably influenced by all these traditions of exegesis.

To the early Christians Jesus Christ was the fulfilment of God's promises to the Jews (Matt. 1.22–23; 2.15, 17–18, 23). But they also used what is known today as 'typology' (in which an event or person in the Old Testament is seen as foreshadowing something in the New). Thus, the writer of the Fourth Gospel sees Moses lifting up the serpent in the wilderness (Num. 21.8f.) as pointing forward to Jesus being lifted up on the cross (John 3.14); Paul sees Adam and Abraham as 'types' of Christ (Romans 4 and 5); and the Jewish Passover is seen as pointing forward to Christ's death (1 Cor. 5.8). There was also allegory (where every item in the story is seen to represent something outside the story). For example, Paul sees Sarah and Hagar (Genesis 16) as referring to the earthly and heavenly Jerusalems (Gal. 4.21–31). More clearly, in Mark's Gospel, the parable of the sower is interpreted allegorically (Mark 4.1–20). Gradually typology and allegory became more and more popular in early Christian exegesis and a number of different writers saw the following connections: the priesthood of Melchizedek (Gen. 14.18) prefigured Christ's priesthood; the 'binding of Isaac' (Genesis 22) and the death of the Passover lamb (Exodus 12) prefigured the death of Christ; the event of the ancient Israelites passing through the waters of the Red Sea (Exodus 14) prefigured Christian baptism; the three visitors to Abraham in Genesis 18 were a revelation of the Trinity; and wisdom in Proverbs 8 was the pre-existent Logos or Son of God.

In some circles all this developed into a flamboyant use of allegory. Many texts of the Hebrew Bible were interpreted allegorically but the interpretation of the parable of the Good Samaritan (Luke 10) by early Christians is perhaps the best-known case. Irenaeus, Clement of Alexandria, Origen and Augustine all have versions of this interpretation. Origen's runs as follows: the man going down to Jericho is Adam; Jerusalem is paradise; Jericho is this world; the robbers are the enemies of man; the traveller's wounds are human sin; the priest is the Jewish Law; the Levite is the prophets; the Good Samaritan is Christ; the beast is the body of Christ; the inn is the Church; the two denarii are knowledge of the Father and the Son; the innkeeper is the angel in charge of the Church; and the return of the Samaritan is the return of Christ at the end of time. Gradually, as this allegorical approach developed into more exotic forms, there was a backlash in some circles. Many stressed the basic coherence or continuing sense of the text they were interpreting rather than plucking out different aspects for allegorical interpretation. Some thought that Scripture had a more literal or historical sense, although not in the modern senses of these terms. They felt a stronger sense of the whole sweep of the text and its straightforward, overall meaning. For example, whereas Origen looked closely for the doctrinal or spiritual meanings of individual words in a text, John Chrysostom can be found trying to ascertain what a particular biblical writer is actually trying to say overall.

The interpretation of Scripture by early Christian theologians varied from writer to writer and different levels were identified, for example the literal, the allegorical and the spiritual or moral. There was often disagreement about how these related to each other and the senses in which they should be understood. While typology and allegory became increasingly popular, all the elements mentioned played an important part in early Christian exegesis throughout the period of the councils. Although the Antiochene and Alexandrian approaches to Scripture had a great deal in common, they exhibited some differences of emphasis, due perhaps to their respective traditions of rhetoric and philosophy. Some of the most important biblical exegetes of the period were: Lucian, Diodore of Tarsus, Theodore of Mopsuestia, John Chrysostom, Clement, Origen, Didymus the Blind and Cyril. Two of these call for particular attention: Theodore of Mopsuestia and Origen.

(d) Representative thinkers:
Theodore of Mopsuestia and Origen

As we have seen, the two Christian theological traditions that began and developed in Antioch and Alexandria produced numerous significant theologians who contributed to thought about Christ in the period of the councils. It was a period of ferocious dispute and contentious controversy. We shall concentrate in this section on one representative thinker from each tradition: the Antiochene Theodore of Mopsuestia and the Alexandrian Origen. Even though both of these were suspect in some of their theological conclusions and both were condemned at later councils, they both represent the basic theological frame of mind of their respective traditions.

Theodore of Mopsuestia (*c.* 350–428) was one of the most significant theologians of the church in Antioch in the fourth and fifth centuries. He grew up at the same time as John Chrysostom (*c.* 347–407), who was later to become Bishop of Constantinople, and they both attended lectures by the philosopher Libanius in Antioch. They both embraced the monastic life and wrote commentaries on biblical texts. They were also both taught by Diodore of Tarsus (d. *c.* 390), another important Antiochene thinker. Theodore became a priest in 383 and was made Bishop of Mopsuestia in 392. He is important for two reasons: his biblical interpretation and his Christology. In terms of biblical interpretation, he is best known for his commentaries. He restricted somewhat the idea that Christ is revealed in the Old Testament and believed that the two testaments bore witness to two very different ages of God's activity in history: the revelation of Christ in the New Testament was dramatically new. However, Theodore took the letter of the New Testament texts more seriously, and he found bases for his doctrinal beliefs there much more easily. Above all, he rejected the Alexandrian allegorical method of interpreting biblical texts, sticking to a much more straightforward approach.

Theodore's approach to the Bible is also evident in his Christology: the distinction between the divine and the human is clear and the humanity of Jesus is stressed. One of his key works, which we know about only through quotations from critics of his theology, is his *On the Incarnation* in 15 books. There are different interpretations of Theodore's Christology and for a long time he was thought of as a 'Nestorian before Nestorius' because, it was claimed, he separated the two natures in Christ as Nestorius allegedly did later. Recent discussion, however, has shown that this judgement might be unfair on both of them. Part of the problem has been that Theodore has been quoted out of context and, as with Nestorius himself, the truth is probably rather different from what has often been thought. Some scholars now see Theodore's Christology as much more orthodox and sometimes even as foreshadowing Chalcedon. But others stress an emphasis or tendency in his thinking that is at least typically Antiochene even if not actually Nestorian. In his attempt to focus on the salvation brought about in Christ, Theodore sees Christ as both thoroughly divine and thoroughly human. As he reacted in the middle of the fourth century to questions about salvation arising out of both the continuing Arian crisis and the emerging Apollinarian crisis, he quickly affirmed both the full divinity of the Logos and the full humanity of Jesus. His emphasis on the humanity of Jesus is noticeably strong, however, and he includes a human rational element in Christ, which Apollinarius denied. He writes of the 'assumed man' Jesus and emphasizes Jesus' individual historical particularity. It is sometimes argued that Theodore was somewhat more Aristotelian than Platonist in his basic approach, emphasizing the particular humanity of Jesus as opposed to a more abstract notion of humanity typical of Platonism and of some Alexandrians. There is not really enough evidence for this claim but he certainly did emphasize

Christ's humanity. He also wrote of the Logos' presence in Jesus as occurring by God's 'good pleasure' or 'good favour' (*kat' eudokian*) and used images of the Temple in which God dwelt in Jerusalem, of man and wife, and of the human body and soul in order to illustrate his understanding of the incarnation. It is partly on these grounds that Theodore has sometimes been accused of adoptionism. Another problem is that he sometimes refers to the Father and the Son as if they are wholly separate entities. Whatever the truth about Theodore's Christology, it was later judged to be inadequate and was condemned (along with Origenism) at the Second Council of Constantinople in 553. In any case, while not all Antiochenes thought exactly the same thing, the overall Antiochene mindset is clearly illustrated in Theodore's approach to his biblical and christological work.

When we turn to the Alexandrian tradition for a representative figure, Origen (*c*. 185–*c*. 254) is the obvious choice. He is the best example of an Alexandrian whose theology was fundamentally Platonist or dualistic and other-worldly. We know of his life from Eusebius of Caesarea's *Ecclesiastical History*, written in the fourth century. Origen grew up during the persecution of Christians under the Emperor Decian and his father Leonides was martyred during that period. It seems that at a young age Origen's enthusiasm for his faith was so great that he wanted to go out and get martyred like his father. Eusebius tells us that his mother hid his clothes so that he could not go out. Another well-known story from Eusebius which arose from Origen's early understanding of Scripture is that, taking Matt. 19.12 literally, he castrated himself, an act that prevented his ordination for years to come because priests were supposed to be physically whole. Whatever we make of Eusebius' accounts it certainly looks as though Origen's enthusiasm for his faith was unusual.

Origen was one of the greatest theologians of the early Church and arguably the most important before the Council of Nicaea in 325. His theology has been interpreted in many different ways but one key problem is that many of his works were translated from the Greek into Latin by Rufinus (*c*. 345–411), who was not always faithful to the original, and survive today only in those versions. Origen's significance lies in three areas: biblical, philosophical and theological. However, it is in his combination of these areas that his real contribution lies. He was, first, a biblical theologian and translator, as witnessed by his famous *Hexapla* (a version of the Bible containing six different translations in parallel columns) and by his many commentaries on biblical books. In his biblical interpretation the Alexandrian allegorical method can be seen very clearly. Second, his theology was philosophical. Like the Jewish theologian Philo of Alexandria, Origen combined biblical interpretation with philosophical speculation. Both were Platonists in the sense that their philosophical theology was thoroughly rooted in the version of Plato's philosophy current in the early centuries of Christianity. As we have seen, the theology of Alexandria was dominated by the concept of the 'other world' and contained fundamentally dualistic notions of the universe. Third, Origen's theology was thoroughly rooted in notions of the Trinity and of the incarnation. In addition to all this he was a master of spiritual theology and mysticism. Origen was thus the first systematic, philosophical, biblical and spiritual theologian of the period.

Origen's theology begins with the being of God himself. This already indicates the basic climate of his theology. His understanding of God is thoroughly trinitarian although there was no fully worked out system of trinitarian theology in his time. For Origen, God the Father (*theos*) is absolute perfection and the Logos, Word or Son is a 'second God' (*deuteros theos*). The Son is one with the Father but distinct from him. The Holy Spirit is also central to Origen's understanding of God. One of the quickest ways to appreciate Origen's theology is to approach it through one of its alleged weaknesses. He was later accused of 'subordinationism', that is, regarding the Logos as a lesser being than the Father. The distinction which Origen emphasized between the two was certainly to feed into later Arianism. But he also taught the 'eternal generation' of the Son, that is, the idea that the Logos was eternally generated in the life of God and therefore was not a creature created by God. The ideas of 'subordinationism' and 'eternal generation' in Origen's theology have earned him the title of 'father of Athanasius and Arius' because the roots of both their theological systems can be found in his.

Like most theologians of the day, Origen believed in the pre-existent Father, Son and Holy Spirit. In addition to the three persons of the Trinity existing before creation, Origen believed that all the souls that eventually became embodied in human beings pre-existed with God. Many of these souls moved away from God and 'fell' from God. In order to save these souls God created the universe. However, another very special soul in eternity became so close to the Logos or Son that it became united with it. This is the root of the incarnation, and therefore of salvation, in Origen's thinking. The Logos and the soul then became incarnate in Jesus of Nazareth and the purpose of this was to draw all souls and all creation back into union with the Father in a predominantly spiritual process of salvation.

Origen's theology was certainly oriented in a Gnostic direction and the various Gnostic groups of the time had systems very similar to his. Origen's theology was also to influence a great deal of later spirituality concerning the return of the human soul to God in the 'other world'. In any case, Origen's system was typically Alexandrian in that the key events and the significance of the incarnation and of the return to God were all fundamentally dualistic and other-worldly. The focus of the incarnation is the life of the Logos and there is little real interest, for example, in the humanity of Jesus, especially in the modern sense. The 'Origenism' that gradually developed out of Origen's theology and that pushed some of the features of Origen's thinking to their logical conclusions was condemned at the Second Council of Constantinople in 553.

This Alexandrian approach was often in stark contrast to the Antiochene tradition, which emphasized Jesus' humanity, and his historical setting and significance. Both traditions raised serious questions about human salvation. The Alexandrians spoke of the humanity of Jesus being 'swallowed up' in the Word or Logos, while the Antiochenes emphasized his humanity, sometimes at the expense of his full divinity. But if the Word did not really become human or if the human Jesus was not really divine, how could human salvation occur through the incarnation? As we shall see in subsequent chapters, this was a question that was to dominate the whole period of the councils. It is worth pausing here to assess its significance.

(e) Salvation

We have already observed that the early Christians thought of Jesus as their 'saviour'. His name means 'the Lord saves'; they experienced him as playing a key role in their new relationship with God. As we have seen, the word 'saviour' conjured up ideas of helping, protecting, delivering, liberating and making safe both physically and in terms of human wholeness. Salvation was to become one of the key issues in the controversies surrounding the councils, whatever the ostensible topic. Unlike the relation between the divine and the human in Christ, however, it was never given a single definition and Christians always used a variety of images and metaphors to illustrate how they thought Jesus had saved them. Salvation was often understood as freedom from sin, but it was thought of in much broader terms as well.

The Apostle Paul used words such as reconciliation (2 Cor. 5.19), redemption (Rom. 3.24; 1 Cor. 1.30), adoption (Gal. 4.4–6) and justification (Rom. 3.23–25) to try to capture his understanding of how Jesus had saved us. Ideas of deliverance (Rom. 11.26) and freedom or liberation (John 8.32; Rom. 8.2), among others, also played a part. In the second century, Irenaeus (*c.* 130–*c.* 200) used Eph. 1.10 as a basis for his theology of 'recapitulation', claiming that Christ 'recapitulated' or 'summed up' (Greek *anakephalaiosis*) the whole of creation in his life, death and resurrection, thereby redeeming humanity and restoring its relationship with God. Augustine of Hippo (354–430), basing his theology on Genesis 3 and Rom. 5.12–21, maintained that humanity 'fell' from original perfection into sin as a result of Adam's disobedience, and that in Christ's life, death and resurrection God provided the possibility of redemption from that fall. Many writers of the period focused on the loss or defacement (caused by sin) of the image of God in human beings (Gen. 1.26). In Christ, they claimed, the image was restored. Athanasius, for example, likened this restoration to the cleansing or repainting of a portrait: Christ came to clean up the image of God in humanity that had been obscured by sin. Very often the focus of the Christian idea of salvation was on Christ's death as a sacrifice (Rom. 3.25), a ransom (Mark 10.45) or a defeat of the devil (Heb. 2.14–15) and these New Testament images contributed to the development of later theories of the 'atonement' (the 'at-one-ment' of God with humanity). There were even theories that God had deceived the devil in Christ. Gregory of Nyssa (*c.* 330–*c.* 395), for example, uses the image of bait on a fish-hook: Christ is the bait, while the devil is the fish. Similarly, Augustine has the image of a mousetrap: Christ is the bait in the trap, while the mouse is the devil!

The metaphor that came to dominate the Christian theology of salvation in many writers of the period of the councils, however, was that of 'divinization' (Greek *theosis*). This idea has its roots in 2 Pet. 1.4, which speaks of Christians becoming 'partakers of the divine nature', and is implicit in the Gospel of John, where Jesus identifies his followers wholly with himself in relation to the Father (chs 14—17). The concept soon grew into a significant, though not clearly defined, image. The basic idea, as the verse in 2 Peter suggests, is that in Jesus, Christians 'partake' of the very nature of God. Later writers who used this verse saw Christians as 'participating' in the divine life of the Trinity through baptism and the eucharist, thus transforming their corrupt nature into incorruption. This process was variously understood, being for some a simple 'participation' in the divine nature, while for others, perhaps, it was even a 'deification'. In any case, it resulted in a substantial physical and spiritual change.

Many writers on Christian spirituality and prayer during this period rooted their ideas in the notion of *theosis*: as the soul approached God through prayer and the mystical 'way of unknowing' (the *via negativa* or 'negative way') it participated in the divine life and so became united with God. Clement of Alexandria was probably the first to use the word *theosis* and we have seen the idea of the return of human souls to God in Origen's thinking. The concept of divinization can also be found in Athanasius, the Cappadocian Fathers and Cyril of Alexandria, among others. In this scheme, salvation is thought of as being made possible by the incarnation of the eternal Logos or Son in Jesus of Nazareth. The whole process is captured succinctly in the well-known phrase found in various forms in a number of writers of this period: 'God became man so that man might become God.' This picture of salvation, in tune with the Platonist tendencies of the period, has remained especially prominent in the theology and devotion of Eastern Orthodox Christianity.

From this material, and the discussion of Theodore of Mopsuestia and Origen in the previous section, it can be seen that there was a wide variety of understandings of salvation during this period. The idea of *theosis* and the return of the human soul to God was especially present in the Alexandrian tradition. The Antiochenes tended, perhaps, to emphasize the incarnation of the Son in the particular human life of Jesus as the moment of salvation. In spite of some differences, however, there was a great deal in common. The question of how Jesus had saved humanity naturally remained important to Christian theologians throughout the period of the councils. But, as we shall see, even though it was a driving force in the surrounding controversies, it was never the main subject of discussion at the councils themselves. The concern with how Jesus had saved human beings obviously gave rise to the basic question of how he was related to God in the first place and it was Christology, not salvation, that became the specific focus of the councils (even though the two are ultimately inseparable). In the following chapters the continuing importance of salvation will be underlined periodically but the main focus will be on Christology.

(f) Conclusion

By the beginning of the fourth century the stage was already set in the Christian communities of the Mediterranean world for what was to emerge later in the christological controversies and ecumenical councils of the Church. Some of the theological distinctions were yet to be made but the basic bricks with which the Christology of the councils was to be built lay ready and waiting. Basically, two traditions of approaching the question of how divinity and humanity were related in Jesus dominated Christian theological thinking. They are usually associated with the two cities in which the traditions grew up: Antioch in Syria and Alexandria in Egypt. There had been eminent individuals in both cities, such as Theodore of Mopsuestia and Origen of Alexandria, who had led the way in theological thinking about the Trinity and the person of Christ. The two cities themselves had important histories, were centres of Christian learning and culture, and were located in significant places. In fact Antioch was to decline in significance in terms of the christological controversies and Constantinople was soon to take its place as the representative city of Antiochene theology. Nevertheless, the two traditions were established. Not mutually exclusive by any means, they had different approaches to the same problems and eventually ended up with different emphases and different solutions. As we have seen, the basic problem can be viewed from a philosophical angle. Alexandria was certainly to become dominated by Platonism in the centuries in which the seven councils were held. The Alexandrians looked primarily to the 'other world', to the world 'beyond' this world. Their thinking about the Trinity and Christ began and ended in the 'other world'. Their interpretation of Scripture bore this out: it was allegorical and often somewhat otherworldly. Antioch, even if still predominantly Platonist, was rather different. It focused more on 'this world' and on humanity, especially in the case of the natures of Christ. The Antiochene approach to biblical texts was much more straightforward.

The first-century concern to find the right language for Jesus' relation to God had now developed considerably and philosophical categories were now also being used in order to clarify it further. By the beginning of the fourth century both Antiochenes and Alexandrians certainly saw Jesus as Lord, Saviour, Son of Man, Son of God and Christ and he was now even more the 'pre-existent Word' or 'Wisdom' that God had used as his instrument in creation and salvation. By this period, however, the New Testament senses of these terms had developed in different directions. Indeed, in many respects Christ was already thought of as both divine and human but the question remained as to how exactly the elements of his identity related to God and to each other. The question of human salvation, conceived increasingly in the East as participation in the life of God, also bore strongly upon the debates from now on. For if Christ were neither truly divine nor truly human, how could he really save human beings?

In the early fourth century a priest called Arius, addressing a matter left somewhat obscure by Origen, popularized the view that the Logos or Son who became incarnate in Christ was not eternally one with God. It soon became clear that a general council of the Church would be needed to address this matter. From now on, the history of the Eastern Church, by far the more dominant wing of the Christian world, is peppered with councils, a feature which is noticeably less evident in the West. The Council of Nicaea was called in 325 to consider Arius and Arianism, the controversy named after him.

3

There was when he was not
The Council of Nicaea (325 CE)

The Council of Nicaea in 325 was called by the Emperor Constantine and is known today as the first ecumenical council of the Church. Although there had already been many local church councils before 325, Nicaea was very different and marks a turning point in Christian history and especially in trinitarian theology and Christology. Questions of how the Father, Son and Spirit were related had emerged already in the second century but the quest for the most appropriate language to speak about Christ and the salvation experienced through him now entered a new phase. Of course, Jesus was already established as Lord, Saviour, Son of God, Son of Man, and Christ, and as the pre-existent Wisdom and Logos, but the precise status of the Logos or Son in relation to God had not yet been clearly spelt out. It was at the Council of Nicaea that the Son who had been claimed to be incarnate in Jesus of Nazareth was proclaimed as co-eternal with the Father. At Nicaea the divinity of the Son and, therefore, of Christ was established and put into written form in the words of a creed.

In order to appreciate the Council of Nicaea it is important to understand the historical context in which it took place. Constantine the Great had recently come to power as Emperor of Rome and the social, political and religious life of Christians in the empire had changed beyond recognition. The new emperor had embraced the Christian religion for both personal and political reasons and had recently announced that the hitherto illegal religion was now legal. In the early years of his reign he was faced with trying to unify the Church as well as the empire. Arius, a priest in Alexandria, was teaching that the Word of God, the Son, even though pre-existent, was not eternal and was, therefore, less than God. Alexander, Bishop of Alexandria, and Athanasius, his assistant, opposed Arius, claiming that the Son was eternally part of the divine nature. The key issue was salvation: if the pre-existent Son were not one with the Father, how could he bring salvation to humanity even if he became incarnate in

Jesus? And how could salvation depend upon someone who was not eternal and not fully divine? The Council of Nicaea was called primarily to address the problem of Arianism, although it also addressed other matters such as the Melitian Schism, the question of when Easter should be celebrated and numerous disciplinary matters relating to church practice and administration. Constantine had hoped that the whole Church, East and West, would be represented at the council but in the event it turned out to be a largely Eastern affair. In order to set the historical scene for the Council of Nicaea we must turn first to Constantine the Great.

(a) Constantine the Great

Constantine the Great was the first Christian emperor and one of the most significant emperors of the period of the councils. His reign marks a radical turnaround both for the Roman Empire and for Christianity. Constantine was proclaimed emperor in the western half of the empire at York in 306 when his father Constantius Chlorus died. But Constantine was still not sole emperor and also still had rivals in the West. In 312, he defeated Maxentius, the ruler of Rome, at the Battle of the Milvian Bridge. This turned out to be an event that changed the course of the history of the Church. Just before the battle, Constantine had a vision that was to affect the history of the Roman Empire. The story of this vision, and thus of Constantine's conversion to Christianity, is told by a number of ancient historians, including Eusebius of Caesarea and Lactantius. No one is certain of the historicity of the events described by these writers but the story is well known. Eusebius' account in his *Life of Constantine* tells how on the day before the battle, while praying, Constantine saw, in a vision in the sky, a sign depicting a cross of light with the words 'In this sign you will conquer' (*in hoc signo vinces*). That night he had a dream in which he was told to use this sign in all his campaigns. Lactantius, in his *On the Deaths of the Persecutors*, has a different version of the story in which Constantine has a dream the night before the battle in which he is told to mark the shields of his soldiers with the cross bent over at the top, probably signifying the *labarum* or *chi-rho*, that is, the first two letters of Christ's name in Greek, ΧΡ. Christian tradition has conflated these two accounts but it seems that the next day Constantine went into battle and was victorious.

After the battle, Constantine ruled in the West while Licinius ruled in the East. Relations gradually deteriorated and Licinius continued to persecute the Christians. Eventually Constantine defeated Licinius in a battle at Chrysopolis in 324 and became sole emperor. His actions in the years that followed were to change the status of Christians and of Christianity beyond recognition. There has been a great deal of speculation about Constantine's own faith, largely because he was not baptized until years later as he lay dying. In fact, this was common practice at the time as it was widely held that serious sin after baptism could not be forgiven and people needed to prepare their souls directly to encounter God. In any case, Constantine embraced Christianity and began to use it to cement his empire together.

It is essential to make a clear distinction between Christianity before Constantine and Christianity after Constantine. As is widely known, pre-Constantinian Christianity was subversive and potentially against Roman law. Before Constantine's legalization of the religion there had been nearly three centuries of intermittent persecution of Christians in which hundreds of people had been martyred for their faith. In a number of waves of persecution during the reigns of the emperors Nero, Decian, Valerian and Diocletian, Christians had been put to death for a variety of reasons. For three centuries before Constantine, Christians were greatly misunderstood. They were accused, for example, of cannibalism because they spoke of eating Christ's flesh and drinking his blood at the eucharist, and also of atheism because they did not believe in any of the recognized gods of the Roman Empire. Also, their refusal to recognize the emperor as divine meant that their civic loyalty was suspect. Struggling for both religious and social identity, Christians were often marginalized, tortured and martyred.

When Constantine became emperor, however, all this changed dramatically. When Constantine and Licinius ruled together they came to an agreement that Christianity would be legal. Tradition has it that this was marked by the so-called Edict of Milan of 313. In fact, this doesn't seem to be an 'edict' as such and some have doubted that it has any connection to Milan, but there is a letter preserved by Lactantius and Eusebius that comes from this date and speaks of religious tolerance. As adherents of a legal religion, Christians were no longer at risk from persecution and abuse. They were now able to get better jobs and had much more influence and status in society. With the help of his mother Helena, Constantine also began to initiate building projects all over the empire, in Rome, Constantinople and in the Holy Land in Jerusalem and Bethlehem. Most important at this stage, Constantine adopted the city of Byzantium in 330, making it a key city in the empire and renaming it after himself: Constantinople or the 'city of Constantine'. This became known as the *nova Roma* or 'new Rome' and took on much of the significance that Rome itself had had. Within a few years Christianity had changed from being a subversive religion whose adherents were frequently put to death, to a legal religion adopted by the state with all the trappings of power, wealth, large buildings and ceremonial. Later, under Theodosius I (emperor from 379 to 395), Christianity became the official religion of the empire and other religions became illegal.

Before Constantine could get a grip on ruling his new empire, however, he faced serious problems. He needed to unite the Eastern empire with the West but he soon found that he had inherited a serious problem in the Church: the teaching of a priest called Arius. This was a threat to the peace and stability of Constantine's regime and immediate action was essential.

(b) Arius and Athanasius

Arius (*c.* 260–336) was born in Libya. The tradition that he studied with Lucian in Antioch and was therefore influenced by Antiochene theology probably has little basis in historical fact. In any case, during the early years of the fourth century he was appointed as a priest in the docklands area of Alexandria known as Baucalis and was popularizing his views about God and Christ by singing songs he had written himself (the *Thalia*). There have been many different views of what Arius taught and most of what we know about him today has been interpreted through the later and more systematic Arianism that developed after his lifetime and continued for several centuries. His views have mostly been represented by his opponents and very little of his own words survives, so it is notoriously difficult to establish the detail of his own teaching.

In spite of this, an outline of Arius' main claims is discernible. He was concerned, above all, to assert the unity of God. Like the Jews, he professed belief in the one God of Abraham, Isaac and Jacob and believed that a monotheistic theology was essential to Christianity. Indeed, not surprisingly, there were occasions when Christians were accused of believing in two or even three gods in the light of their claims about the Father, Son and Holy Spirit. Arius' beliefs about God obviously affected his beliefs about Jesus. If the Christian God was the God of Judaism, then how exactly was the Son related to God? On the basis of some rather informal hints in the New Testament, like the baptismal formula in Matt. 28.19, trinitarian theology had already begun to develop in the second century in the theology of thinkers such as Irenaeus, Clement and Tertullian (*c.* 160–*c.* 225). The fourth century was to see many further developments in the Christian understanding of the Trinity. Christians were keen to affirm their strong belief not only in one God but in his son Jesus Christ whom, as we have seen, they experienced and perceived to be closely related to God. Their experience of the Spirit in their lives was also an extremely powerful element. All this had led to Christians sometimes speaking as if there were three gods or three aspects of the one God. As we have seen, the language of Wisdom, Logos and Son had been used to try to articulate something of their experience in these respects. Turning what had been poetic images into formal philosophical statements was not easy and some even felt that this was a mistake.

In his powerful assertion of God's ultimate unity, then, Arius was also by implication saying something about the Son. Because only God can be God, he claimed, the Son must be secondary. This idea can already be found in Origen's theology in the third century and it is in this sense that he is the 'father of Arius'. As noted in the previous chapter, Origen had called God *theos* and the Son *deuteros theos* or a 'second God'. Arius taught that although the Son who had become incarnate in Jesus was pre-existent, he was not co-eternal with God and was therefore a creature. The Son was indeed with God before the creation of the universe and was in this sense pre-existent. But because only God was eternal and 'ungenerated' or 'not made', his Son must have come into existence at some point (or 'time') before time itself was created. Whether he ever actually uttered it or not, the following catch-phrase about the Son indicates something of Arius' view: 'there was [a time] when he was not' (*en pote hote ouk en*). The degree to which Arius distinguished between God and the Son is much disputed but it is clear that the distinction was there. If the Son who became incarnate in Jesus was ultimately only a creature and was on the side of creation and of creatures, the question arose as to whether this creature, like God's other creatures, could sin and fall away from God. (Indeed, the radical Arians Aetius and Eunomius, in the later fourth century, claimed exactly this.) Furthermore, Arius used biblical texts such as John 14.28 to support his case: 'the Father is greater than I'. In Arius' theology there turn out to be two 'Lords': both the Father and the Son whom he created. But if the Son is ultimately only a creature, however special and however pre-existent, the question of his role in the salvation of humankind is raised. How could a creature who is not one with God offer human beings salvation? Indeed, the issue of salvation soon became central to the whole Arian controversy and was a key concern of Arius' chief opponent, Athanasius of Alexandria.

At the time of Arius' rise to fame in Alexandria, Athanasius (*c.* 296–373) was a young deacon at the cathedral there. In the early years of the fourth century he too was becoming well known and may already have been writing his famous work *On the Incarnation of the Word of God* (*De incarnatione verbi dei*), although some scholars believe that this was written later. This work does not mention Arianism but Athanasius later wrote a considerable amount specifically against the Arians, for example his *Four Discourses Against the Arians* (*Contra Arianos*). In much of what he said and did in the early stages Athanasius represented his bishop, Alexander of Alexandria, and between them they asserted an incarnational, trinitarian theology which countered Arius' views. In some ways Arius' teaching can be seen to be more conservative than that of Athanasius and he is increasingly portrayed in this light today. Even though there were different opinions emerging on the Trinity, it was clear to many that God must be eternally one and that the Son must be secondary. In contrast, Athanasius' teaching can be seen as more radical and innovative. He saw the eternality of the Son as fundamental to salvation. For him, the Son that had become incarnate in Jesus was not simply a creature created by God at some 'moment', even before he created time and the universe, but was actually eternally one with God himself. The Son was 'eternally generated' by God and was thoroughly part of God himself even though also distinct from him. For Athanasius, there never was any kind of serious gap between the Father and the Son, never a time when the Son did not exist and was not one with the Father. It is in this respect that Origen (with his doctrine of the eternal generation of the Son) was the 'father of Athanasius'.

Like Arius, Athanasius used biblical texts to support his case. Most of the texts and concepts we considered in Chapter 1 were used and cited by Athanasius in his discourses against the Arians. The titles we considered, such as Son of God and Son of Man, now mostly taken to be referring to the divinity and humanity of Christ, also played their part. The key thing to note, however, is Athanasius' use of Scripture. Certainly John 1.1, Hebrews 1, Philippians 2, and Colossians 1 are all used to emphasize the eternal nature of the Son or Logos. But Athanasius also uses Old Testament texts extensively in reference to the co-eternal nature of the Son and it is clear that for him Christ is prefigured in the texts of the Hebrew Bible. Thus, Proverbs 8 and the concept of God's wisdom, used extensively in this debate, is used by Athanasius to affirm the pre-existent oneness of the Son with the Father. References to the 'light' and the 'kingdom' (Pss. 45; 144; 89 and 90) are also linked up to the eternal nature of the Son. And texts like Jer. 1.6; Mal. 3.6; Baruch 4.20, 22 and Susanna 42 (a book in the Apocrypha and part of the Greek version of the Bible) are also used. It was, of course, the Fourth Gospel that provided Athanasius with the most useful texts: 'the Word was with God, and the Word was God' (John 1.1), and 'I and the Father are one' (John 10.30). The interesting thing is that although the Arians also used biblical texts to support their case (and sometimes the same texts, e.g. Proverbs 8), the more radical Athanasius sometimes seems to fail to see their more obvious Arian meaning. On the face of it, for example, Prov. 8.22, relating to 'wisdom', has an obviously Arian meaning when applied to the Son: 'The Lord created me at the beginning of his work, the first of his acts of old.' But Athanasius saw the emphasis lying on the pre-existence of the Son, on his eternal unity with God and on his 'eternal generation'. Of course, everything depended on the presuppositions of the person using the text and on the implied meaning of individual words and phrases. It is quite clear, in any case, that Athanasius stood firmly in the Alexandrian tradition of interpreting scriptural texts in a very open and flexible, allegorical manner and saw the co-eternal nature of the Son with the Father as thoroughly scriptural. It is important to realize that most of these theological issues simply did not arise in the culture of the time in which the New Testament books themselves were written.

As Arius' following grew and as the doctrinal and political dimensions of the controversy deepened it was soon realized that a serious division was occurring in the Church. The controversy was not only about the interpretation of Scripture but also about the status of the Son, the nature of God the Trinity, and human salvation. Some thought of salvation in predominantly spiritual terms while for Athanasius it also had a serious physical dimension: the Son or Logos had become flesh, thereby saving physicality itself from corruption. The issues in the debate were couched in terms of Platonist philosophy, focusing on the 'other world', but there was often a serious concern with the physical world as well. To modern ears the controversy often sounds abstract and obtuse but for fourth-century Christians the focus was very much on the 'real world' of God and Christ and (for some) on the physical aspects of salvation: only God can save, they thought, so if the Son who has saved us was not fully divine then the salvation of the whole world is void.

It is impossible to know the numbers, but a variety of different groups emerged at this time with many conflicting shades of theological opinion. When Constantine the Great became sole emperor in 324 he soon realized that he would need to take control of the Arian controversy and make a move towards bringing the various factions together. It soon became clear that a general council, the first time such a body had been called, was

---

Historical excursus 3: Nicaea

Ancient Nicaea (modern Iznik in Turkey) was important before the council was held there in 325. The town may go back as far as the ninth century BCE. In the *Iliad*, Homer refers to a person called Askania who led Phrygian troops from this region. The name of the lake then became Askania. Later, according to the geographer Strabo (first century BCE), a town was founded in 316 BCE by Antigonos I of Macedonia and was, therefore, known as Antigonia. In 301 BCE Lysimachus, one of Alexander the Great's generals, took the town and renamed it after his late wife Nike, hence Nicaea (the Greek 'k', kappa, is transliterated into Latin as 'c'). At this point it became the capital of the province of Bithynia, in which it was situated. It was replaced as capital by Nicomedia, further north-east on the Sea of Marmara, in 264 BCE.

One of the most significant residents of Nicaea in the second century CE was Pliny the Younger, Governor of Bithynia from 111 to 113. He glorified Nicaea and is known to have restored the theatre (which is still visible today) and the gymnasium. It is also well known that during his period as governor he was faced with problems of how to deal with Christians. There was still a great deal of misunderstanding over who the Christians were at this time and Pliny wrote to the Emperor Trajan in 112 asking him what to do with them. The reply came back that the Christians were not to be sought out but that if they were a nuisance they were to be punished. This

---

needed in order to address the problem and to try to heal the theological divisions that had opened up. Constantine was also concerned to bring the two halves of his empire more firmly under his control. With these concerns in mind, he called a council in 325, originally to be held in Ancyra (modern Ankara in Turkey) but actually held in Nicaea, where Constantine had a beautiful summer palace on the edge of a lake. This provided an attractive and convenient setting for the council.

(c) The Council of Nicaea

The Council of Nicaea took place from 20 May to 25 July 325. It was probably one of the most splendid occasions of the ancient Church. Nobody

exchange between Pliny and Trajan has become a celebrated case in the development of imperial attitudes towards Christians in the early centuries and it is clear that at this point they were still not perceived as enough of a problem to be tracked down for punishment. Thus it was from Nicaea, the residence of the governor, that the letter was sent to the emperor. In the same period, Nicaea became popular as a centre of artistic and literary activity. Shortly after the rule of Pliny there was an earthquake (in 123) which destroyed the city. It was rebuilt by the Emperor Hadrian. In the third century the town was once more destroyed and rebuilt.

Nicaea is doubly important for the history of the councils. In addition to the council called by Constantine the Great in 325, the Second Council of Nicaea was called by the Empress Irene in 787 and dealt with the iconoclasm controversy.

Situated on the edge of the beautiful Lake Nicaea, the town is dominated today by mosques. Some of the remains of Constantine's palace, where the first council was held, can be seen. The location of the Second Council of Nicaea was the sixth-century Byzantine Church of the Holy Wisdom built by Justinian. This was destroyed by an earthquake in the eleventh century although some parts of it remain. The building seen today was built in the eleventh century. It was eventually turned into a mosque and a minaret and mihrab were added. It is now a museum.

knows for sure how many bishops attended but it was probably about 300. The council is often known as the 'council of the 318 fathers' but this number comes from Hilary of Poitiers (*c.* 315–367/8) later in the fourth century and is not based on any serious knowledge of the number of people present. Constantine refers to there being about 300 present and this was later connected with Abraham's 318 trained men in Gen. 14.14. The significance of this number is, therefore, typological rather than historical. Eusebius of Caesarea says there were 250 bishops present. The real number is probably somewhere between 250 and 300. Constantine had hoped that there would be bishops from all over the world but in the event there were very few from the West and the council turned out to be a largely Eastern affair. Pope Silvester I did not attend because of age and

Figure 2 Lake Nicaea with the remains of Constantine's summer palace on the left, Iznik, Turkey. Location of the First Council of Nicaea (325 CE)

ill-health but he sent two representatives from Rome. There was one bishop from Italy and Hosius of Cordova from Spain, whom Constantine appointed as his own Western adviser. There were bishops from Gaul, Illyria, Africa, Crimea, Armenia, Persia, Egypt and Asia Minor. The key characters other than the emperor were, of course, Alexander, Athanasius and Arius; Eusebius of Caesarea, originally on the Arian side; Eusebius of Nicomedia; Marcellus of Ancyra; Eustathius of Antioch; and Paulinus of Tyre. One tradition says that Nicholas, Bishop of Myra in Asia Minor, attended the council. He later became Saint Nicholas and later still, his name was corrupted to Santa Claus! According to this tradition, as the Council of Nicaea was in session and Arius was presenting his case to the assembled bishops, Nicholas strode forward and slapped Arius across the face because of his views!

No account of the council survives from the event itself but there are a number of texts that give some idea of what it might have been like, including: a letter of Constantine sent to various churches after the council; Eusebius of Caesarea's letter to his church in Caesarea concerning the creed that had been accepted at the council; and material from Eustathius of Antioch and from Athanasius of Alexandria. The main source, however, is *The Life of Constantine*, written by Eusebius of Caesarea over a decade after the council. Eusebius was Bishop of Caesarea in Palestine and played a key part in the council. Indeed he was a close ally of Constantine and preached the sermon at his funeral in Constantinople in 337. Eusebius' account of the Council of Nicaea is not an 'objective historical account' in the modern sense and is clearly written to build up a dramatic sense of the importance of Constantine and the council and of how unifying and successful an event it was. But in any case, Eusebius gives an interesting outline of events and it is worth following his account briefly. He describes how Constantine called the council and invited many bishops, even offering them help with their travel arrangements. He then tells how bishops came from various parts of the world, naming the participating countries as if the event were another Pentecost (Acts 2). Indeed, Eusebius says that the Council of Nicaea was more important than Pentecost.

When it comes to the actual occasion, according to Eusebius' account, the bishops are gathered together in the imperial palace in Nicaea in order of rank. As everyone waits in silence, members of Constantine's family enter, followed by the emperor himself. Eusebius says that Constantine enters in glorious apparel of gold and precious stones like a messenger from God. He then waits for a golden chair to be brought out and after receiving a sign from the bishops sits down. The whole assembly is then seated. Next, one of the bishops, we are not told who (perhaps Eusebius of Caesarea or Eusebius of Nicomedia), stands up and reads a speech of thanksgiving to God. Then the emperor himself rises and gives his speech in Latin, the formal language of the empire. The speech is a request for peace and unity and Constantine says that strife in the Church of God is worse than war. He then opens up discussion of the various views represented and a violent uproar immediately breaks out. Constantine is able to calm everyone down through his use of Greek and brings the council to agreement and order. Following the main sessions of the council, participants attend events celebrating the twenty years of Constantine's reign and the proceedings go on well into the summer. It is impossible to know how historically reliable Eusebius' account is but it gives a vivid sense of what the occasion might have been like.

In addressing the Arian controversy and other matters the participants in the council produced a creed or statement of faith. We shall call this the 'Creed of Nicaea'. It was the main result of the council and expresses what became known subsequently as 'Nicene orthodoxy'. Before turning to look closely at the creed it is worth observing that Eusebius says that it was Constantine himself who suggested that a particular word be used in the creed to try to heal the theological divisions at the council. Crucial philosophical distinctions come into play here. The word suggested by Constantine was *homoousios*. It was to be used for the relation between the Father and the Son. This was a term that had originally been used by the various Gnostic groups and in Latin by Tertullian in the West (*consubstantialis*) but it had not been used particularly in the East. It is often surmised that Constantine, whose Greek was limited, got the idea of using the word from Hosius of Cordova. In any case, it was to become the heart of the theology of the council and of the subsequent debates about Christ. The word *homoousios* meant 'of the same substance' or more literally 'of the same stuff'. In fact there is an element of ambiguity in this word because even though two things might be made 'of the same stuff' that does not mean that they are identical or one and the same. It can mean that they are made from the same type of stuff. This ambiguity was quite useful as it left room for a distinction between the Son and the Father to be affirmed as well as a unity. The word was therefore used in the Creed of Nicaea.

(d) The Creed of Nicaea

The creed produced at the Council of Nicaea is often called the 'Creed of Nicaea' in order to distinguish it from the Niceno-Constantinopolitan Creed, the creed popularly known today as the 'Nicene Creed' and recited by Christians at the eucharist. That creed has significant additions on the Holy Spirit and will be discussed in the next chapter. The concern here is with the original 'Creed of Nicaea', its statements of belief in God and Jesus, and its clauses deliberately aimed at Arius and his followers. Of course, the idea of a creed or a statement of belief did not originate with Nicaea. In the early Christian attempts to find the most appropriate language to use of Christ certain 'credal' sentences had emerged. Such statements can already be found in the New Testament. In Matt. 28.19 Jesus tells his disciples to baptize in the name of the Father, Son and Holy Spirit, a trinitarian structure that foreshadows later creeds. Paul writes that 'Christ died for our sins in accordance with the Scriptures, that he was buried, that he was raised on the third day' (1 Cor. 15.3f.), and elsewhere, that Christ was 'descended from David according to the flesh' (Rom. 1.3f.). Even the basic 'Jesus is Lord' (1 Cor. 12.3) might be seen as credal. Of course, these are not 'creeds' in the later sense but they are fragmentary statements of belief that can be seen to foreshadow the later Creed of Nicaea.

There are also second-century writers in whose works a credal shape can be discerned, for example Ignatius of Antioch, Irenaeus and Tertullian. These writers indicate a threefold belief in the Father, the Son and the Holy Spirit in texts that were used in questioning candidates for Christian baptism. Later, the fragments and threefold structure developed into longer creeds. The Old Roman Creed, for example, was used in the context of baptism in Rome from the end of the second century and became the basis of the later Apostles' Creed. It was in the early Christian initiation ceremonies that the idea of a full statement of belief first emerged. The need at that time was not so much to have an apologetic statement of faith against unbelievers as a statement of faith for use in baptismal liturgies. Nevertheless, the need to have a statement of faith in Christ was fundamentally the same need that had given rise to the early use of the titles Lord, Saviour, Son of God, Son of Man, and Christ. Even though it emerged in the context of theological controversy, therefore, the Creed of Nicaea stands in a long tradition of titles, expressions and short credal statements that summarize Christian faith. It is thought by many scholars that Eusebius of Caesarea put forward a basic creed at Nicaea that he had brought with him from his church in Caesarea in Palestine and that this creed formed the basis of the creed that was accepted by the council. However, others maintain that another creed, possibly from the Jerusalem church, lies behind the Creed of Nicaea.

In any case, the creed produced at Nicaea runs as follows (differences from Eusebius' creed are indicated in italics):

We believe in one God the Father All-sovereign, maker of all things visible and invisible;

And in one Lord Jesus Christ, the Son of God, *begotten of the Father*, only-begotten, *that is, of the substance of the Father*, God of God, Light of Light, *true God of true God, begotten not made, of one substance with the Father*, through whom all things were made, *things in heaven and things on the earth*; who for us men and for our salvation *came down* and was made flesh, *and became man*, suffered, and rose on the third day, ascended into the heavens, is coming to judge living and dead.

And in the Holy Spirit.

And those that say 'There was when he was not,'
and, 'Before he was begotten he was not,'
and that, 'He came into being from what-is-not,'

or those that allege, that the son of God is

'Of another substance or essence'

or 'created,'

or 'changeable'

or 'alterable,'

these the Catholic and Apostolic Church anathematizes.

(Bettenson and Maunder 1943/1999, pp. 27–8; italics theirs)

With the background to the Council of Nicaea in mind it can easily be seen how the different clauses of the Creed of Nicaea came about and what they were intended to mean. First, 'creed' comes from the Latin word *credo*, meaning 'I believe'. In fact the original Greek of the Creed of Nicaea has the plural 'We believe' as its opening words and is a statement of corporate faith. Originally in the context of a baptismal liturgy creeds were in interrogatory form ('Do you believe . . . ?'). Only later, in the councils, do we find the purely declaratory form as above. Like some of its fragmentary predecessors, the Creed of Nicaea divides into three affirmations of belief: in God; in Jesus Christ; and in the Holy Spirit, although hardly anything is said about the Spirit. This was to be added later in the Niceno-Constantinopolitan Creed. Nevertheless, the Creed of Nicaea does have a basic threefold, trinitarian structure. Finally, and not surprisingly, there is a whole paragraph at the end of this creed deliberately aimed against the alleged teaching of Arius. The various sections of the creed require separate attention.

First of all, belief in God the Father was fundamental to the early Christians. The fathers of Nicaea, on all sides, wanted to affirm belief in the one God of the Old Testament, the God of Abraham, Isaac and Jacob. Not only was he creator of the physical universe as in the book of Genesis, but also of the invisible world. Everything that exists, they believed, came into being as a result of the supreme power of the one God. The Greek sense of the one ultimate God beyond the many gods also came into this theology. The second affirmation turns to Jesus Christ. Jesus Christ is seen as the one and only Lord and Son of God. The original significance of these expressions has been outlined in Chapter 1 and although their senses had evolved somewhat in the light of theological and philosophical developments, they now appear as part of the basic affirmation of Nicene faith. But now Jesus Christ is also 'only begotten of the Father' and 'of the substance of the Father'. This is where the difference from Arius can perhaps be seen most clearly. The language is aimed against Arius and affirms Christ's supreme relation to the Father. He is the only begotten Son who is eternally begotten and who has the same substance or essence as God. The expressions 'God of (or 'from') God' and 'Light of (or 'from') Light' are now used. Jesus Christ the Son of God is indeed one with God and with the Light, bringing to mind the opening verses of the prologue to the Fourth Gospel. And then, specifically against Arius again, Jesus is 'begotten not made'. He was not created as Arius claimed, but has the same substance as the Father and is eternally begotten. Here, as has already been pointed out, the word *homoousios* is used. This non-scriptural word worried a number of bishops at Nicaea and after. But most of those at the council concluded that the word really did express what they wanted to say and was continuous with the faith of the New Testament writers.

Jesus Christ is also the one 'through whom all things were made'. The word 'Logos' is not used here but the Logos, God's instrument of creation, is implied (cf. John 1.3; Col. 1.16). In this creed, Jesus Christ the Lord and Son of God is actually the one who is God's instrument of creation, creator of things both heavenly and earthly. Next Jesus Christ is the one who for the sake of human salvation came from heaven and was united with flesh. The emphasis on salvation is noteworthy, since this lay at the heart the whole Arian controversy and the entire Council of Nicaea. Then, bringing to mind the prologue to the Fourth Gospel again, the creed claims that the heavenly Christ became united with humanity. In Greek, the word for flesh (*sarx*) means 'the whole human condition' and the word translated 'man' (*anthropos*) means humanity generally rather than 'male'. Here, in effect, is John 1.14 with the full emphasis on incarnation and salvation. The next clauses of the second section follow the life of Jesus, stressing the importance of his earthly existence, his suffering, his resurrection and ascension, and his final return at the end of time.

Finally, without any comment, there is a simple affirmation of belief in the Holy Spirit. This abrupt ending signifies the lesser importance of the Holy Spirit in Greek theology at this time, but also indicates that the focus of the Council of Nicaea was Jesus Christ. The Holy Spirit already figured in Christian experience and belief but the controversy about its status *vis-à-vis* God and Christ was to spring up more clearly after Nicaea and was to be one of the key issues at the later Council of Constantinople in 381. At Nicaea, only the bare affirmation of belief in the Spirit was necessary. It is interesting to note that the Virgin Mary is conspicuous by her absence in this creed whereas she appears in the Old Roman Creed. The controversies over her status in God's plan of salvation were addressed later at the Council of Ephesus in 431. Far more important at Nicaea was the focus on the status of the Son and the need to anathematize the supposed views of Arius once and for all, hence the specific, lengthy attack on these views at the end of this creed. Anyone who claimed that there was (a time) when the Son did not exist or that he was created or was of another substance from God, or that he changed at all, is anathematized or condemned.

Thus, the fathers of the Council of Nicaea stated in credal form everything they wanted to say about the nature of the Father and the Son, even if the creed was thin on the Holy Spirit. Although there are different views on the matter, it is possible that it was this creed, with later additions on the Holy Spirit, that subsequently became known as the 'Nicene Creed' or the 'Niceno-Constantinopolitan Creed'. It did not get into the liturgy for some time to come and only finally became established in Rome in the eleventh century. But the Creed of Nicaea was the Council of Nicaea's profession of faith and was to all intents and purposes the theological outcome of the council. It has been regularly recited in its revised form by Christians for centuries.

In addition to the Arian controversy there were some other matters that called for attention at the Council of Nicaea. One was the so-called Melitian Schism in Egypt; another was a controversy over the date of Easter. There were some practical matters that needed addressing too.

(e) The Melitian Schism

The Melitian Schism concerned the status and treatment of Christians in the Egyptian church who had lapsed during one of the persecutions before Constantine became emperor. Although it is sometimes difficult to get a clear picture of what Christians had to do in this period to get arrested, it is clear that while some withstood temptations to deny Christ, others gave in. In the 'Great Persecution' of Diocletian, for example, in the early fourth century, some Christians handed over Scriptures to be burnt, while others performed the so-called 'sacrifice test', a ritual of offering sacrifice to pagan gods or to the emperor, thus in effect denying Christ. Indeed, there were different degrees of denial of Christ but the issue that arose for the Christian communities was what to do with those who had lapsed in their faith but who wanted to be admitted back to the main community later when the persecution was over. Some wished to return to Christ while others claimed that their denial had been a mere formality in order to avoid arrest. For some leaders in the Church the question arose as to what measures should be taken to readmit such people and whether or not they should be rebaptized. Those who lapsed in their faith became known in the West as *lapsi* or *traditores* (Latin *traditor*, 'traitor', 'betrayer' or 'hander-over' of Christian books).

Constantine had already had to deal with a similar problem in third-century Africa before he became sole emperor. A schism there, known as 'Donatism', had arisen out of a rigorist approach to those who had lapsed. The Council of Nicaea did not address Donatism but it was confronted with the Egyptian version of the problem, the Melitian Schism. In Egypt, Melitius, Bishop of Lycopolis, took exception to the liberal policy of Peter, Bishop of Alexandria, concerning the lapsed. Peter, according to Melitius, was allowing them back into the Church too easily. Melitius then started to ordain his own clergy and a schism gradually developed. The Council of Nicaea discussed the matter and it was decided to acknowledge the Melitian priests as long as they operated under the Bishop of Alexandria. The sect continued as a separate body, however, down to about the eighth century. A similar problem known as Novatianism, which had originally arisen in the Roman church in the third century, was also discussed at the council and received a similar response.

(f) Celebrating Easter

Another controversy that was addressed at Nicaea concerned the date of Easter. At least two different dates were observed, resulting in considerable conflict. The basic question was this: when, in relation to the Jewish Passover, should the Christian celebration of Easter take place? Jesus' death and resurrection had taken place at the time of Passover, so the resurrection was closely associated with that festival. The theological connections between the two events were important. For Jews, Passover celebrated freedom from slavery in Egypt. For Christians, Easter celebrated freedom from sin through the death and resurrection of Jesus. The Jewish Passover was celebrated on the fourteenth day of the Jewish month of Nisan. Many Christians, therefore, claimed that the resurrection of Jesus should be celebrated on the same day. But Jesus' resurrection had occurred on a Sunday, so the question arose as to whether Easter should be celebrated on the following Sunday rather than on 14 Nisan itself.

The Christian communities in Asia Minor mostly kept to the date of the Jewish Passover. They became known as the Quartodecimans (from a word meaning 'fourteen'). However, those who disagreed and wanted to keep Easter on the following Sunday did just that. They lived mostly in the West and especially in Rome. Their view was that even though Easter was still related to Passover, it should now have a degree of independence.

Indeed, when Christians from Asia Minor visited Rome they wanted to keep Easter in their own way at their own time and because there were already different liturgical practices, conflict had arisen. In 155 CE, Polycarp, Bishop of Smyrna, tried to encourage Christians in Rome to keep Easter on 14 Nisan, but failed. Later in the second century Pope Victor excommunicated Polycrates, Bishop of Ephesus, over the issue.

But in addition to all this, there were differences between Antioch and Alexandria concerning the calculation of the actual date of Easter: in Antioch they celebrated it at the time of the Jewish Passover, whereas in Alexandria they always celebrated it after the spring equinox. At the Council of Nicaea, again in an attempt to bring unity to the Church, it was decided that Easter should be celebrated on a Sunday and that the Alexandrian calculation of the date should be followed. In spite of this, however, practice continued to vary and the Quartodecimans remained a distinct group down to about the fifth century.

(g) The canons of Nicaea

In addition to addressing such problems as the Melitian Schism and the date of Easter, the Council of Nicaea found itself faced with numerous practical issues that had arisen in the churches of the time. In response to these, the council produced twenty 'canons' or statements that have survived:

1 Those who have castrated or mutilated themselves cannot be in the clergy. If others have done it to them and they are worthy they may be ordained.
2 Those who have just joined the Church cannot become priests and bishops straight away.
3 Bishops, priests and deacons should not have women living with them (apart from wives in cases of married clergy) except a mother, sister, aunt or anyone else 'above suspicion'.
4 A bishop should be consecrated by all the bishops in a province or at least by three.
5 Those who have been excommunicated by one bishop should not be received back by another. There should be a synod (local council) twice a year to deal with this.
6 The Bishop of Alexandria has authority in Libya and Pentapolis. The Bishops of Rome and Antioch have similar authority over their own

metropolitan areas. If anyone is made a bishop without the agreement of the Metropolitan, he is not legitimate.

7 The Bishop of Aelia (Jerusalem) should have the authority due to him, and the Bishop of Caesarea should have his.

8 The clergy of the Novatian sect (sometimes known as Cathari, meaning 'pure' – it was a Western version of the Melitian teaching) can remain in the clergy. If there is a catholic bishop in a city he is to take precedence over the Novatian bishop and Novatianists should do a period of penance.

9 If anyone has been ordained without examination or has confessed to serious sin, then he is not validly ordained.

10 If anyone has been ordained and then has lapsed he should be deposed.

11 Those who have fallen away without compulsion should be treated kindly and given a period of penance.

12 Those who have been arduous but have fallen away must do a period of penance.

13 Those who are lapsed and are about to die can be given communion but if they recover they can only join in the prayers, i.e. the first part of the eucharist but not communion.

14 Lapsed Christians coming back into the Church should spend three years with the catechumens.

15 Bishops, priests and deacons should not move from one city to another.

16 Those who have moved should not be accepted. Those ordained in another place are invalidly ordained, and those persisting in another place should be refused communion.

17 Clergy participating in usury should be struck out of the clergy.

18 Deacons should not give the eucharistic elements to bishops and priests or receive them before they do. They should receive after the more senior clergy. Anyone who disobeys should be struck out of the diaconate.

19 Paulianists (followers of the teaching of Paul of Samosata) should be rebaptized and/or re-ordained when they return to the catholic Church if they are worthy, otherwise they should be deposed.

20 Prayer should be made standing on Sundays and during Pentecost.

With these twenty canons, the Council of Nicaea attempted to implement a degree of unity and common practice among the churches of the fourth century. It is clear that there was a significant need for greater organization and administration, especially regarding matters of morality, authority and general practice. The issue concerning the ordination of eunuchs or anyone who had mutilated himself is interesting and arose because it was felt that those who were ordained should ideally be physically complete. This idea was derived from the rules for Jewish priesthood found in Lev. 21.16–24. Origen's self-castration comes immediately to mind here and clearly this practice had become a problem. There were obviously also sexual scandals over clergy living with women to whom they were not married and marriage itself was not encouraged. Standards concerning this needed to be set. There had been cases of people ascending the ecclesiastical ladder far too quickly and becoming bishops when they had not long been Christians. There were obviously many cases of groups splitting away, of people who had lapsed in some way, and of crises over who was in charge and how to administer and manage the churches. There needed to be clearer guidelines over 'who was in' and 'who was out' and it is obvious that penance played a part in the return of those who had lapsed. The direction that prayer should be made standing up is interesting; it derived from Jewish practice but also obviously symbolized the resurrection. In all of these canons it is clear that the Church of the fourth century was struggling to clarify its own sense of identity and practice. The process of drawing clearer lines concerning the Church's own internal practice and administration was now well under way.

(h) Conclusion

The Council of Nicaea was the most momentous event in the history of the Christian Church up to that time. Nothing like it had occurred before. The Christian quest for the most appropriate language and the most useful philosophical categories with which to speak and think of the relation between the Son and the Father, and of human salvation, had turned a significant corner. Something approaching 300 bishops gathered at Nicaea and produced a statement of faith, the Creed of Nicaea. Some very important theological matters were addressed. The Melitian Schism and the date of celebrating Easter were also discussed and the council responded to numerous practical problems with its twenty canons. In addition, the Council of Nicaea inaugurated an 'age of councils' that was to continue for centuries. It had been called by the emperor himself, thereby establishing councils as vehicles of imperially guided decision-making for the Church. Perhaps more significantly still, the Council of Nicaea established a sense of the difference between right and wrong belief, and therefore of the difference between 'orthodoxy' and 'heresy' – a sense, it was felt, that was important to the Church as a whole.

After the council the Arian controversy raged on and a variety of different forms of Arianism emerged. In the later fourth century appeared the radical Arians, Aetius and his pupil Eunomius, who separated the Son from the Father even more than Arius had done. According to Athanasius and Rufinus, some ten years after the council Arius himself was taken short in the street in Constantinople, dashed into a public toilet, and died suddenly. This story may be the result of Arius being likened to Judas (cf. Acts 1.18). Athanasius became Bishop of Alexandria in 328 and lived several decades longer but his views did not always prevail. He was sent into exile from his city and see five times for an overall period of twenty years in the half-century after the council. On one occasion, as the police pursued Athanasius in a boat down the River Nile, he turned around and began travelling towards them. They asked the steersman if he had seen 'the traitor Athanasius', and Athanasius replied, 'He is not far.' The police continued their search! The controversy continued and the stories are numerous.

The Council of Nicaea is often presented as 'solving the Arian problem'. It did no such thing, for the situation was much more complex than that. All but two bishops signed the statement of faith at Nicaea but many more were unhappy with its outcome. One story has it that some participants inserted an iota into the word *homoousios* in copies of the creed that they signed, making it *homoiousios*, meaning 'of like substance' rather than 'of the same substance'. They wanted a broader range of belief about the relation between the Father and the Son than had been allowed at the council. The word *homoiousios* certainly entered the debate later. In the middle of the century Athanasius wrote his *On the Council of Nicaea* (*De Decretis*), in which it is clear that there were still anti-Nicaeans who expressed serious concern that the word *homoousios* was non-scriptural. The word *homoios* or 'like' was another word used in the debate, mostly by those who rejected the language of 'substance' altogether and who wanted to affirm an even greater ambiguity in the relation between the Father and the Son. But there were limitations to this word too. Paulinus of Antioch famously commented that 'the Kingdom of God is like a mustard seed – but not much!', drawing attention to how unlike things that are 'alike' can be.

Questions of identity and distinction in the relation between the Father and the Son continued to be debated. On a number of occasions, such as the Council of Sirmium in 357, the Arian view of Christ prevailed over

Athanasius' views and over 'Nicene orthodoxy'. The theology of the creed produced at Sirmium was Arian and Hilary of Poitiers called it 'the blasphemy of Sirmium'. The Emperor Constantius (joint emperor from 337; sole emperor, 350–61) condemned Athanasius and supported the Arians. Challenging the Nicaeans but also exiling the extreme Arians Aetius and Eunomius, Constantius supported the use of the word *homoiousios*. Interestingly, issues relating to the status of the Son were still so much part of everyday concern in Constantinople in the later fourth century that Gregory of Nyssa commented that even when one went out and asked the price of bread or went to the baths one would be told that the Father was greater than the Son or that the Son was made out of nothing! Such issues may have been of less interest, one suspects, in outlying areas.

Whatever is made of all this, it is clear that the Council of Nicaea was a beginning rather than an end. It remains a serious question whether Arius' Christology was so clearly wrong. He is appreciated increasingly by modern scholars as a theologian in his own right and his position certainly made a serious point. Why could a semi-divine creature not be God's agent of salvation upon Earth? The answer at Nicaea was that God himself had been experienced as acting in Jesus and only God himself could bring salvation to human beings. Overall, the Council of Nicaea had focused on the nature of God as Trinity; on the relation of the Son to the Father; on finding the most adequate language to use of that relation; and on the crucial question of human salvation. The Son had been pronounced 'of one substance with the Father'. The divinity of the Son, and therefore of Christ, had effectively been established. But in addition to provoking continuing questions about these matters the council raised a new set of concerns: what about the Holy Spirit? And how exactly did the divine Logos or Son relate to the humanity with which it became united in the incarnation in Jesus of Nazareth? Along with the continuing Arian controversy, these questions formed the focus of debate in the years that followed Nicaea and especially at the second ecumenical council, held at Constantinople in 381.

4

Of a rational soul and a body
The Council of Constantinople (381 CE)

In the decades that followed the Council of Nicaea, the question of the relation between Jesus Christ and God the Father continued to press itself upon theologians. And some new dimensions of the problem also emerged – namely, the questions of the Holy Spirit and of Apollinarianism. Constantine the Great died in 337 and was buried with great splendour in the Church of the Holy Apostles in Constantinople. By this stage he had gained status as the 'thirteenth apostle'. But his attempt to unite the empire and the Christian world can hardly be said to have been a success. Even though Nicaea was to become established as the first ecumenical council of the Church and was quoted with the utmost respect at future councils, it is clear that in many ways there was no more unity in the Church after the council than before it. Arius' popularity grew and Athanasius' declined at times. Constantine himself on occasion supported Arius and the Arians more than Athanasius when it suited him.

There was no doubt now, of course, that Jesus was Lord, Saviour, Son of God and Christ or that he was the Wisdom of God and the eternal, pre-existent Logos or Son. But many Church leaders were dissatisfied with the outcome of Nicaea. Even though a creed had been formulated and various documents and beliefs agreed upon, there were still those who felt a sense of unease with the council's decisions. As we have seen, the non-biblical *homoousios* still seemed inadequate to some and in the middle years of the fourth century there were still those who preferred to use *homoiousios* or *homoios* in order to express a greater distinction between the Father and the Son. Centuries later, Edward Gibbon (1737–1794), in *The History of the Decline and Fall of the Roman Empire*, commented on how ridiculous the disputes over a 'single diphthong' looked to later readers! So much did Arianism gather momentum in the fourth century that the biblical scholar and translator Jerome (*c.* 345–420) said that 'The whole world groaned and marvelled to find itself Arian' (Kelly 1958/2003, p. 238). In general, Christianity continued to grow rapidly and under Theodosius

---

Historical excursus 4: Constantinople

Constantinople (modern Istanbul in Turkey) was the most important city in the East during the period of the councils. It had existed before Constantine as a much smaller city whose name was Byzantium (Greek 'Byzantion'). In the fourth century CE Constantine the Great founded it as the main city of his empire and rebuilt it, naming it 'Constantinopolis', that is, the 'city of Constantine', after himself. In the days before Constantine the city was far less important. Its situation on the Bosphorus was advantageous in all sorts of ways and Byzantium already had a notable history stretching back to about the thirteenth century BCE. The origins of the actual city are usually traced to the seventh century BCE (*c.* 658), when tradition has it that Byzas from Megara in Greece founded it on the Golden Horn. A group of Athenians and Megarians from Greece consulted the oracle at Delphi and were told to go and occupy the European side of the Bosphorus 'opposite the land of the blind' (Chalcedon) and establish a city there. Previous settlers had occupied the Asian side and were said to be blind because they had apparently not seen the advantages of the European side. In the second century CE the Roman emperor Septimius Severus destroyed Byzantium only to rebuild it later and name it Augusta Antonina after his son.

When Constantine took the city in 324, it bore no resemblance to Rome. However, his dream was to have a 'new Rome' in the East that would become what the old Rome had long been in the West. Constantine therefore developed the city and made it the seat of his newly established Christian empire. It was dedicated on

---

I became the official religion of the Roman Empire in 380. Other religions were now forbidden and Christianity's relation to the state was cemented much more firmly.

In addition to the persistence of Arianism two other issues also became central. First, there was the essentially trinitarian question of the relation of the Holy Spirit to the Son and to the Father. Second, there was a more specifically christological question: if the Son had been established as 'of one substance with the Father' at Nicaea, how did that eternal Son actually relate to the humanity with which it became joined in its incarnation in Jesus of Nazareth? On the first issue, the Holy Spirit had always

4 November 328 and remained the capital of what was by then the eastern empire until 1453, when the city fell to the Ottoman Turks under Mehmet II. Constantine's Constantinople thus became larger and more significant than Byzantium had ever been.* But during Constantine's lifetime it was never what it later became under Justinian. Constantine transformed the city by putting in new walls and building churches. He probably did not build the first Church of St Sophia; that was to fall to his son, Constantius. But he built the original Church of St Irene, where the Council of Constantinople was held in 381, in addition to the Church of the Apostles, where he was eventually buried in 337. He also enlarged the Hippodrome, started by Septimius Severus, which was to become the scene of many notable events in the history of the city. The Church of Hagia Sophia, which still remains today, was built by the Emperor Justinian in the sixth century and the city grew even more.

Constantinople was the setting of three of the seven ecumenical councils: one in 381 (dealing with questions of the Holy Spirit and Apollinarianism), and two smaller councils in 553 (dealing with the 'Three Chapters Controversy') and 680–1 (dealing with Monothelitism).

---

* The word 'Byzantium' has only been used by historians of the whole empire founded by Constantine since the nineteenth century. In its day the city was seen as part of the Roman Empire and its inhabitants as Romans.

been part of Christian experience in worship and in everyday life but it was now important to establish in philosophical terms whether the Spirit should be seen as divine or not. Here, exactly parallel questions to those that had arisen over the status of the Son emerged: was the Spirit co-eternal with the Father and the Son, or was it created by God? The Cappadocian Fathers – Basil of Caesarea, Gregory of Nazianzus and Gregory of Nyssa – were to make significant contributions towards answering this question. In relation to the christological question, Apollinarius, Bishop of Laodicea, suggested that Christ had no real human mind and that the Logos had taken its place. The Council of

Constantinople was called by Emperor Theodosius I in 381 to deal with these issues. It reaffirmed the faith of Nicaea against Arianism; effectively established the divinity of the Holy Spirit (although this is widely debated); and announced that Apollinarius' understanding of the relation between the divinity and humanity of Christ was inadequate in terms of human salvation.

(a) The Holy Spirit

As trinitarian theology developed during the decades after the Council of Nicaea the question of the status of the Holy Spirit became more and more important to Christian theologians. Of course, there is no doubt that the Spirit had played a key part in Christian experience from the very beginning and was perceived as a crucial dimension of God's presence in the world. The question that now emerged was how that Spirit was to be seen in relation to the Father and the Son. Christians knew that they were not the first to experience the Spirit. It had been a powerful force in the Jewish experience of God for centuries. Indeed, the Spirit (Hebrew *ruah*) had moved over the waters of creation in the book of Genesis (1.2); it had rested on particular individuals and given them strength to serve God (Judg. 3.10); and it had been the driving force behind Israel's prophets (Isa. 61.1; Mic. 3.8). Christians believed that the same Spirit continued to act in Jesus and in the Church. It had descended on Jesus at his baptism (Matt. 3.16; Mark 1.10; Luke 3.22) and in Nazareth (Luke 4.18; cf. Isa. 61.1) and had been poured out on the community on the day of Pentecost (Acts 2.4). In John's Gospel the Spirit is called the 'paraclete' (Greek *para*, 'alongside', and *kaleo*, 'to call', and hence 'advocate' or 'comforter') and plays a particular role in the Christian community after Jesus' departure (e.g. John 14.15–17; 20.21–22). Throughout the following centuries Christians continued to experience the Spirit influencing their lives and they needed to develop a coherent 'pneumatology' (Greek *pneuma*, spirit, and *logos*, word, hence 'words about the Spirit' or 'doctrine of the Spirit').

Questions inevitably arose as to whether the Spirit that Christians experienced was really 'divine' or whether an evil spirit might sometimes be active. Some felt, in any case, that it was too much to claim that the Spirit they experienced was equal to God or that it should be accorded the same status as the Son. Indeed, it was in this context that Christians were sometimes accused of believing in two or three gods. Some began to see real dangers in claiming that the Spirit was equal to the Father and the Son and began to fight the very idea of the 'divinity of the Spirit'.

Others, like Athanasius, had already in the early fourth century spoken of the '*homoousion* of the Spirit', claiming that the Spirit was indeed 'of the same substance' as the Father. In the middle of the fourth century the Cappadocian Fathers, especially Basil, led the way in defending the divinity of the Holy Spirit. They were three of the most dynamic figures in the Church of their day and their theology of the Holy Spirit contributed significantly to the Council of Constantinople.

(b) The Cappadocian Fathers

The Cappadocian Fathers were Basil of Caesarea (*c.* 330–*c.* 379), Gregory of Nazianzus (329/30–389/90) and Gregory of Nyssa (*c.* 330–*c.* 395). They are known as the 'Cappadocian Fathers' because they came from Cappadocia in central Asia Minor. Basil and Gregory of Nyssa were brothers, whose sister Macrina founded a monastic community and was an able theologian in her own right. Her Life was written by Gregory of Nyssa. Gregory of Nazianzus was their friend. Basil was a churchman, politician and statesman. He came from a wealthy, aristocratic background and studied at the university at Athens, where he met Gregory of Nazianzus. Basil wrote widely on a number of different theological subjects and was well known as a preacher in the diocese in which he was bishop. One of his best-known works is his *Homilies on the Six Days of Creation*. It is his work on the Holy Spirit, however, that we shall be most concerned with in this section. Gregory of Nazianzus was different. A quiet, withdrawn man, he was primarily a poet and a monk. He was ordained somewhat reluctantly and eventually became Archbishop of Constantinople, but soon left in search of solitude. Gregory of Nyssa was different again. He had a daughter and may have been married. His theological writings, like *The Life of Moses*, are more mystical than those of the other two. Along with Athanasius and John Chrysostom, Basil of Caesarea and Gregory of Nazianzus were both recognized very much later as 'doctors of the Eastern Church'. Gregory of Nyssa's theology was always considered too mystical for him to be admitted into such company! Although the Cappadocian Fathers' contributions to theology were quite different, together these constitute one of the most important elements in the determination of Christian orthodox thinking in the fourth century. Not only did they write on issues concerning the Holy Spirit, but they also addressed christological questions arising out of Arianism and Apollinarianism.

In order to understand the significance of the Cappadocian teaching on the Holy Spirit, it is important to appreciate their contribution to trinitarian theology generally and their place in the wider context of the debate in the fourth century. As we have seen, the Arian controversy over the divinity of the Son had in fact been one aspect of a wider trinitarian controversy, a controversy over the relation between the Father and the Son rather than specifically over Jesus. Issues relating to the nature of God continued to arise and the concern over the Spirit was inevitably part of that. Questions about God, the Son incarnate in Jesus, and the Spirit soon became intertwined and answers to questions such as 'how did Jesus relate to God?' and 'what is God like?' had long separated Christians from both Jews and pagans. Christians were at pains to point out that they still believed in the one God of Judaism. They were keen to remain mono-theists like their forefathers. But they still wanted to affirm the close rela-tion of the Son and the Spirit to the Father and to Jesus. Questions of the inner nature of God therefore soon emerged. In the second century Christians were already asking whether God was eternally three or only three in separate aspects of his relation to the world. On the one hand, God could be seen as basically and eternally simply one. This was one early view and it claimed that God went out from eternal unity and took on other 'modes' in relation to creation. He became 'Logos' or 'Son' in his role as creator of the world and 'Spirit' in his role as redeemer and inspirer, and would return to his basic unity at the end of time. This view is known today as 'Modalism', as it saw the different aspects of God's being as dif-ferent 'modes' of his existence. Sabellius in the early third century re-presents this line of thinking. However, there were others who wished to assert eternal distinctions within the Godhead and to claim that God was eternally three, and not just three in his relations with the world, for it seemed axiomatic that God is unchanging, one and the same. For exam-ple, Origen spoke of the 'eternal generation of the Son'. The Cappadocian contribution to the Christian idea of the Trinity lay in their affirmation of the distinctions within the unity of the Godhead. They opposed Arius and reaffirmed the theology of Nicaea. For them the Son was both one with the Father but also eternally distinct. They also opposed the theo-logy of Apollinarius of Laodicea and affirmed Jesus' full humanity in the incarnation.

When the question of the nature of the Spirit arose, the issues were more or less parallel to those that had arisen concerning the Son. Was the Holy Spirit a creature or was it eternally one with the Father and yet also eternally distinct from the Father? A further question now also arose: how was the Holy Spirit related to the Son? The key Cappadocian response to these questions came from Basil of Caesarea in his work *On the Holy Spirit.*

Basil had been criticized by various people because of some doxologies he had used in worship. Apparently he had used two versions interchangeably: 'Glory to the Father, with the Son, in the Holy Spirit' and 'Glory to the Father in the Son through the Holy Spirit'. His usage of the words 'in', 'through' and 'with' was accused of inconsistency and the question soon arose as to what the difference really was and whether it mattered. In *On the Holy Spirit* Basil claims that it does not matter and that both doxologies are all right. Basil's critics disagreed. They claimed that there were differences and that in any case the Holy Spirit was not 'of the same substance' as the Father. Basil's key opponents were those whom he called the 'Spirit fighters' or Pneumatomachoi, i.e. those who claimed that the Spirit was only a creature and should not be placed on a level with the Father. Athanasius had maintained the '*homoousion* of the Spirit' against the so-called Tropici (a group of 'Spirit fighters' that allegorized biblical texts), who claimed the same thing as the Macedonians (named after another fourth-century 'Spirit fighter', Macedonius). In relation to the particular words used of the Spirit, the Pneumatomachoi claimed that 'with him' indicated equality, whereas 'through him' indicated subordination. Basil affirms the equality of substance of Father, Son and Holy Spirit, thus affirming the divinity of the Spirit, although it is well known that he never quite says openly and straightforwardly that the Spirit is divine.

Basil considers the Holy Spirit in the light of Scripture, worship and philosophy. He uses Scripture frequently to show that there are many ways of talking about the Spirit and that the small words 'in', 'with' and 'through' do not indicate a radical difference in the nature of the Spirit, as his opponents maintained. His critics based their ideas on Aristotelian concepts of causality, maintaining, for example, that the cause does not have the same nature as the effect. Basil shows that scriptural writers used such terms interchangeably of Father, Son and Holy Spirit. More importantly, he claims that because Christians worship the three as one, and are baptized in the name of the three persons, they are indeed united in worship and honour and, therefore, have the same nature. He frequently cites Matt. 28.19, claiming that it shows the unity of the Father, Son and Holy Spirit. For Basil, the three persons of the Trinity are unified but also distinct. Like the other two Cappadocians, he is keen to affirm that he does not believe in three gods, but in one God in three distinct persons. He wishes to avoid reverting to the monotheism of Judaism or the polytheism of the Greeks. He sees the Holy Spirit as pre-existent and co-eternal, part of the Father's instrument in creation. Citing Ps. 33.6, he sees the Holy Spirit's role in creation as crucial: 'By the word of the Lord the heavens were made, and all their host by the breath (spirit) of his mouth.' Because of the Spirit's role in the creative process it is clear that he deserves honour and glory and that his nature is part of the divine nature. For Basil, the Holy Spirit has the role of perfecting creation and of bringing it to completion; he is thoroughly involved in the work of God. The Spirit also enlightens believers. When Christians pray 'in the Spirit' the emphasis might be on their own spiritual life, but when they speak of the status of the Spirit 'with' the Father they are speaking of the Spirit in himself. For Basil, there is a need to avoid giving the impression, as some did, that God had two sons, or that the Spirit was somehow a grandson! So Basil affirms the one nature of the three persons.

Probably for political reasons Basil was economical in his use of language affirming the *homoousion* of the Spirit but the other two Cappadocians went further. Gregory of Nazianzus wrote on the Holy Spirit in his fifth *Theological Oration* and is quite clear: 'What then? Is the Spirit God? Most certainly. Well, then, is he consubstantial? Yes, if he is God' (Hardy 1954, p. 199). And Gregory of Nyssa, discussing baptism in his *Against the Macedonians*, is clear that the Holy Spirit possesses the divine nature and does the work of the Father. In general, the three Cappadocians often stressed the individuality of the three persons of the Trinity even more than their unity. Unlike Augustine of Hippo, who emphasized the unity more, the Cappadocians spoke of the 'co-inherence' of the three persons of the Trinity, a concept that stressed their individuality in relation to each other. The Greek word *perichoresis* was later used of this idea. This overall concern not only with the status of the Holy Spirit but also with the most appropriate language to use for his relationship with the Father provoked another question: where did the Holy Spirit come from or proceed from? This question concerned what is now known as the 'procession of the Holy Spirit'. The answer was that he came 'from the Father through the Son' and this became established as the standard form of expression. Centuries of debate over this language were to follow, of course, but for the moment, all we need note is that the question of the status of the Holy Spirit had been addressed more consistently by the Cappadocians than ever before and that the divinity of the Holy Spirit was now increasingly affirmed by Christians. Although the 'Spirit fighters' saw the Spirit as a creature, the Cappadocians saw him as having the same nature as the Father and the Son. The Cappadocian contribution to the theology of the Spirit and to the theology of the Trinity, therefore, is immeasurable. When the Council of Constantinople was called in 381 the divinity of the Holy Spirit was already fairly well established even if it was not always stated in so many words. This was largely due to the work of the three Cappadocian Fathers.

(c) Apollinarius of Laodicea

In addition to trinitarian questions concerning the status of the Holy Spirit, the mid-fourth century saw the emergence of a specifically christological problem. The focus of attention was on how the divine Logos or Son actually became united with the humanity of Jesus in the incarnation. How did the two natures unite in the one person? Apollinarius of Laodicea (*c.* 310–*c.* 390), sometimes known as Apollinaris (the Greek form), suggested an answer. He was Bishop of Laodicea in Syria and was a staunch defender of the decisions of the Council of Nicaea. In his Christology, he was fearful of allowing Christ two separate personalities and thereby undermining the union between the two natures. His concern was to establish the union of the two natures as firmly as he could. There were, however, two basic questions about 'human nature' to be faced before anything else could be said: of what does it basically consist? And how could Christ's human nature become united with the Logos in Jesus? The notion of human nature dominant in the fourth century and presupposed by Apollinarius can be traced back to Plato. For Plato, human nature consisted of three parts: the body (*soma*); the soul (*psuche*); and the mind (*nous*). Modern people can find it difficult to distinguish between the soul and the mind, but for the ancients the difference was clearer. For Plato, the soul was the vital principle that gave life to human beings and to animals, while the mind was the rational element that distinguished human beings from the rest of the animals. Even if it is seen as part of the soul, it is the rational and directing part. In Apollinarius' day, Plato's basic tripartite psychology was accepted and presupposed: human beings consisted of a body, a soul, and a mind. This tripartite psychology formed a fundamental part of Apollinarius' Christology.

The next questions were what Christ's humanity was like and where and how the eternal Logos or Son fitted in. Apollinarius' basic solution, as far as we can tell because his teaching, like that of Arius, has been preserved largely by his opponents, was that whereas Christ had a body and a soul, the rational element in his make-up consisted entirely of the divine Logos. In other words Christ himself had no human mind (*nous*). If this seems odd, it must be remembered that Apollinarius thought that the eternal, divine Logos completed the necessary elements in Christ's make-up. God was the creator of humanity anyway and provided the distinctive rational element in the incarnation. As creator, God could provide 'perfect humanity', as it were, without there being any shortfall through the lack of a particular human mind. It seems that on these grounds Apollinarius implied the pre-existence of Christ's flesh, driven as it was so fundamentally by the divine Logos. Another implication was that because Christ's mind was divine he was omniscient, so that when the Gospels show him ignorant of when the end of time will come or as hungry or thirsty, he must be seen as simply pretending, in order to accommodate himself to the human condition, like a rich man mixing for a time with poor people.

So all-pervading was the divine Logos in Christ, according to Apollinarius, that his Christology was soon seen as 'docetic' (Greek *dokeo*, 'to seem'). That is, Apollinarius was seen as portraying Christ as only seeming to be human and therefore as undermining his humanity and ultimately, by implication, all flesh and matter. If Christ had no real human mind or *nous* then he could hardly have been a full human being. The lack of a human mind meant that in the incarnation Christ had no distinctive individuality; he was not a particular human being. God had just assumed 'general humanity'. If this were the case, then, as with Arius' teaching, the salvation of humanity was in question. If Christ was not fully human, how could he save human beings from sin? This was precisely the objection of Apollinarius' most famous critic, Gregory of Nazianzus, who pointed out that 'that which he has not assumed he has not healed; but that which is united to his Godhead is also saved' (Hardy 1954, p. 218). If the Logos did not 'assume' or become united with full humanity, said Gregory, full humanity cannot have been healed or saved in the process. As the Council of Chalcedon was to say later, Christ had a 'rational' or 'reasonable soul and a body'. Apollinarius had deprived Christ of a rational soul and therefore of his full humanity. Indeed, he had deprived humanity of its salvation and given us a play-acting Christ the Lord. His teaching was condemned at the Council of Constantinople in 381.

(d) The Council of Constantinople

Like Nicaea before it, the main aim of the Council of Constantinople was to unite the Church through dealing with some of its doctrinal problems. Half a century after Nicaea, Arianism was still spreading. Apollinarianism had appeared and was gathering momentum. Issues concerning the Holy Spirit and its relation to God needed addressing because groups such as the Macedonians and the 'Spirit fighters' were claiming that the Holy Spirit was not God. And there was a need for various disciplinary and general

Figure 3 The Church of St Irene, Istanbul (ancient Constantinople). The Council of Constantinople (381 CE) was probably held in an earlier church on this site

ecclesiastical issues to be addressed too. With a view to dealing with all this, the Emperor Theodosius I called a council that gathered in the capital city in May 381. It consisted of 150 bishops from the East (Asia Minor, Egypt and Thrace) and 36 Macedonian or 'Spirit-fighting' bishops who left the council early. Pope Damasus I of Rome did not attend and did not send representatives. The council met in the Church of St Irene in Constantinople and was presided over by Melitius of Antioch (not the Melitius who gave his name to the schism discussed at Nicaea), who died while it was in session. Gregory of Nazianzus attended and took over when Melitius died. He was not as successful as he had hoped in bringing his theology of the *homoousion* of the Spirit to bear upon the proceedings although the few documents that remain from the council indicate that a broadly Cappadocian theology of the Spirit prevailed. The council also re-affirmed the faith of Nicaea and rejected Arianism and Apollinarianism. It came to rank as 'ecumenical' later, at the Council of Chalcedon in 451.

Perhaps the greatest mystery relates to the creed usually associated with the Council of Constantinople. There have been many different views of this. It was affirmed as the Creed of Constantinople at the Council of Chalcedon but it is not clear whether the Council of Constantinople actually produced it. It is now known technically as the 'Niceno-Constantinopolitan' creed and also popularly as the 'Nicene Creed'. It was once thought to be the original Creed of Nicaea with significant additions, although this view is now widely rejected. Although the new creed may not actually have been produced at the Council of Constantinople, it is usually associated with it and is generally reckoned to sum up its theology, especially on the Holy Spirit. Basically, it is at least a reaffirmation of the theology of Nicaea with additions. It is worth looking closely at the additions, especially the section on the Holy Spirit, and at the broader questions concerning the 'procession' of the Holy Spirit and the later *filioque* clause. First, here is the full text of the Niceno-Constantinopolitan Creed (differences from the Creed of Nicaea are indicated in italics):

> We believe in one God the Father All-sovereign, maker *of heaven and earth, and* of all things visible and invisible;
>
> And in one Lord Jesus Christ, the only-begotten Son of God, Begotten of the Father *before all the ages*, Light of Light, true God of true God, begotten not made, of one substance with the Father, through whom all things were made; who for us men and for our salvation came down *from the heavens*, and was made flesh *of the Holy Spirit and the Virgin Mary*, and became man, *and was crucified for us under Pontius Pilate, and* suffered *and was buried*, and rose again on the third day *according to the Scriptures*, and ascended into the heavens, *and sitteth on the right hand of the Father*, and cometh *again with glory* to judge living and dead, *of whose kingdom there shall be no end*:
>
> And in the Holy Spirit, *the Lord and the Life-giver, that proceedeth from the Father, who with Father and Son is worshipped together and glorified together, who spake through the prophets*:
>
> *In one holy Catholic and Apostolic Church*:
>
> *We acknowledge one baptism unto remission of sins. We look for a resurrection of the dead, and the life of the age to come.*
>
> (Bettenson and Maunder 1943/1999, pp. 28–9)

It is clear from a simple comparison between this creed and the Creed of Nicaea that there are differences and that some significant additions have been made. In general, there are now more details in the section on Christ, and a new section on the Holy Spirit and other matters has been added. Sometimes the change is only in word order but there are also significant new features that are worthy of note: the words 'maker of heaven and earth' are added to the first line and then reworded later; the Son of God is now 'only-begotten' and 'before all the ages' (these ambiguous words, with which Arius in fact agreed, are significantly different from Nicaea's very Athanasian 'from the substance of the Father'); the phrases 'God of God' and 'things in heaven and things on earth' are also reworded; the Holy Spirit and the Virgin Mary have been added and are now involved in the incarnation (see Luke 1.26–35); crucifixion under Pontius Pilate is now specifically mentioned; Jesus is now actually 'buried'; death and resurrection are now 'according to the Scriptures'; Jesus now 'sitteth on the right hand of the Father' and will come again 'with glory' to judge. Then, as a result of the teaching of Marcellus, Bishop of Ancyra, to the contrary, it is stated that Christ's kingdom will have no end (preferring Luke 1.33 to 1 Cor. 15.28). The phrases specifically condemning Arianism in the Creed of Nicaea are now omitted. Even though there are significant differences, the overall effect of all this is to reaffirm the Nicene faith and to fill in the detail. The appearance of Mary in the new version of the creed is especially noteworthy. Her place in Christian theology and worship was developing rapidly at this time and was to cause controversy in the years leading up to the Council of Ephesus in 431. The problems that arose concerning her status will be addressed in the next chapter.

More important here is the additional material on the Holy Spirit. Faith in the Holy Spirit is professed in a new section and some detail is spelt out. The Spirit is now 'Lord' (cf. 2 Cor. 3.17) and 'giver of life' (cf. 2 Cor. 3.6). The Spirit originates or 'proceeds' from the Father (cf. John 15.26) but there is no mention here of the later phrase 'and the Son' (Latin *filioque*). The Spirit is worthy of worship like the Father (cf. Matt. 28.19; 2 Cor. 13.14), perhaps implying divine status, and is the same Spirit that spoke through the prophets of Israel (cf. Acts 28.25). All this can suggest that the Spirit is divine although the word *homoousios* is not used; the language is predominantly biblical.

Following this, there is a section on the Church which is 'one, holy, catholic and apostolic'; on Christian baptism and forgiveness; and a profession of faith in the resurrection of the dead at the end of time, and in the next or other age or world. Doctrinally and in terms of Christian faith, these are important additions and indicate a return to a creed focused more for use at Christian baptism (with its trinitarian focus) than the Creed of Nicaea with all its anathemas.

(e) The *filioque* clause

It is worth pausing briefly here to consider the so-called *filioque* clause. It was added to the creed later in the West and is not found in either the Creed of Nicaea or the Niceno-Constantinopolitan Creed. However, the roots of the idea can be found in Augustine's theology and this eventually helped to make it more acceptable in the West. The actual expression 'and the Son' (*filioque*) appeared in the sixth century in Spain and then became part of the Niceno-Constantinopolitan Creed in the West. It concerns the relations of the persons of the Trinity and indicates something of how the relation between the Son and the Holy Spirit was understood even in the fourth century. The idea that the Spirit proceeds 'from the Father', as the creed claims, raised the question of the 'procession' of the Holy Spirit. By this is meant simply the question of where the Holy Spirit proceeds or originates from. The answer in the fourth century was, of course, 'from the Father' (as John 15.26 indicates) and 'through the Son', and this is the line taken, as we have seen, by the Cappadocian Fathers. However, if the Spirit proceeds 'from' the Father and only 'through' the Son the problem of the subordination of the Son emerges once again. The Father is, to be sure, the source of the Spirit's life. But the implication that the Son, not being part of the source but a mere channel, is therefore less than the Father in status smacked once again of Arius' subordination of the Son, which had already been much debated at the Council of Nicaea and since. Thus the question later arose as to whether the phrase 'and the Son' should be added to the creed in relation to the procession of the Spirit. This indeed happened and the *filioque* clause is now part of the Western Niceno-Constantinopolitan Creed professed regularly by Western Christians.

However, in the East, the notion that the Spirit proceeds from the Son as well as the Father smacked either of Modalism, that is of merging the persons of the Trinity so much that the permanent distinctions are lost, or of a notion of the three persons which sees them as above each other in a hierarchy, which threatens the position of the Father as the foundation and source of unity within the Trinity. The Cappadocians, for example, emphasized the relations between three distinctive persons who were essentially one, rather than the idea of a hierarchy of separate persons. For these reasons Eastern Christians rejected the *filioque* clause and never accepted it into their creed. The procession of the Spirit was not addressed at the Council of Constantinople and still remains an issue that divides Eastern and Western Christians today.

(f) The canons of Constantinople

Like the Council of Nicaea, the Council of Constantinople produced several canons. Only a few survive and some of those which are traditionally attributed to Constantinople probably come from a smaller council of the same period. In the four canons that indisputably come from the council itself, the following concerns appear:

1 There is a strong affirmation of the Council of Nicaea. Some of the different factions that had developed within the Arian camp, for example the ultra-Arians (Anomoeans or Eunomians), who claimed that the Son was nothing at all like the Father, and the Semi-Arians, who claimed that the Son was 'like' the Father, are anathematized. The ordinary Arians (or Eudoxians) are condemned. The Pneumatomachoi and the Apollinarians are also condemned, along with the Sabellians, Marcellians and Photinians.
2 Bishops are not to function outside the borders of their own dioceses without invitation.
3 The Bishop of Constantinople is to become second in importance only to the Bishop of Rome. This reflects the status of Constantinople as the 'new Rome' and its increasing ecclesiastical importance over Alexandria and also Antioch which was receding in importance. Later, at the Council of Chalcedon in 451 the status of Constantinople was raised again.
4 Another issue that had arisen concerned Maximus, a Cynic philosopher turned Christian who was illegally consecrated Bishop of Constantinople in contest with Gregory of Nazianzus when the Arianizing Bishop Demophilus went into exile. The canon declares that Maximus never was a bishop and that those he ordained were not really ordained.

In canons that most likely come from a later council:

1 the divinity of the Holy Spirit is actually affirmed; and
2 other disciplinary matters are dealt with, including a probable reference to another Melitian schism, different from the one dealt with at Nicaea over the lapsed in Egypt. This concerned Melitius, Bishop of Antioch, who, as noted earlier, presided at, and died during, the Council of Constantinople. He was in conflict with another orthodox group of Christians in Antioch.

Once again, these canons indicate the practical concerns of the Church of the time. There were clearly still issues of practice and authority in addition to the main theological issues. These were similar to those already dealt with at Nicaea and indicate little change in the general climate of the Church. They also show how strong the tendency to controversy and division really was in this period: this was no golden age of unity and harmony!

(g) Conclusion

The Council of Constantinople in 381 eventually became known as the second ecumenical council of the Church, though not until 451 when the Council of Chalcedon incorporated the creed associated with Constantinople into its theology and documents. Less is known about Constantinople than about Nicaea, as we have no parallel source to Eusebius' *Life of Constantine* for Constantinople. However, the significance of Constantinople lay in the issues it addressed. It was called primarily to address the trinitarian issues of the day, namely Arianism, the question of the nature and status of the Holy Spirit and the Christology of Apollinarius. The Arian controversy had continued to rage after the Council of Nicaea and Arianism was now once again condemned at Constantinople by the reaffirmation of the faith of Nicaea. The divinity of the Holy Spirit had been established in the theology of the Cappadocian Fathers and it seems likely that this was generally the direction taken by the council concerning the Spirit. However, although documents associated with the council seem to affirm the divinity of the Holy Spirit (the Creed, and the canon rejecting the Pneumatomachoi), it is unclear whether this was the overall view of the council itself. The attempts of Apollinarius to find a satisfactory Christology had also now been condemned. Finally, like Nicaea, Constantinople addressed a number of practical concerns that had arisen in church life and administration generally. The problems addressed at Constantinople were of the utmost significance, although we should not overestimate the council's achievements; those problems continued to be debated.

In the controversies and debates that led up to the Council of Constantinople Christians sought the most appropriate language and philosophical categories in which to articulate their understanding of the relation between the divine and the human in Christ. Trinitarian theology was developing as the Church tried to say clearly what it believed that God had done for human salvation in Jesus Christ and continued to do through the Holy Spirit. But there was still a long way to go in terms of clarifying the details of the incarnation. If the divinity and humanity

78

of Christ were not related in the way that Apollinarius had suggested, then how exactly were they related? What was Christ's role in human salvation? And what specifically was the Virgin Mary's role in the incarnation? Such questions came to a head in the early fifth century and were addressed at the Council of Ephesus in 431.

5

Holy Mary, Mother of God?
The Council of Ephesus (431 CE)

After the Council of Constantinople in 381, new controversies came to dominate Christian thinking about Christ. Even if Apollinarius was wrong, and even if the three persons of the Trinity were all divine and yet distinct, there was still a problem about how the divinity and the humanity in Christ were related. The next debate to dominate the discussion focused on what is known today as 'Nestorianism'. Nestorius was an Antiochene theologian who became archbishop of the increasingly powerful see of Constantinople in 428. The concerns in this debate were once again questions of the Trinity, Christology, language and salvation. As we shall see, Nestorius spoke out against the use of a particular title for the Virgin Mary – Theotokos, often translated today as 'Mother of God' though it is probably better understood as 'God-bearer' or 'bearer of God'. His reservations about this word were based on an insistence that the humanity of Christ should be duly acknowledged both in worship and in theological debate. Addressing Mary as 'God-bearer' gave him the impression that Jesus was not really human. Nestorius' reservations soon provoked anger, especially from Cyril of Alexandria, who perceived Nestorius as trying to separate the two natures of Christ or even deny his divinity. For Cyril, if Mary was not the 'bearer of God' in giving birth to Christ, then Christ was not divine.

By the early fifth century, the cult of Mary was already evident right across the Christian world and especially in the East. The title 'Theotokos' was widely known and loved among the general population of Greek-speaking Christians. From the time of Constantine, churches had been dedicated to Mary, hymns had been written and sung to her and she had come to play an increasingly significant part in Christian worship. Her virginity and example had captured the Christian imagination. She was soon held up as a model of purity and sinlessness and clearly had a special role in God's purposes. It was now clear that views about Mary affected views about Christ. Any claim that Mary was not Theotokos, therefore, was explosive. In spite of Antiochene reservations about this title, therefore, Mary was affirmed as Theotokos at the Council of Ephesus in 431 and again at Chalcedon in 451. Underlying all the debates about the nature of the Son, of Christ and of Mary was the same concern with human salvation that had been present all along. Gregory of Nazianzus had made the point that what was not assumed by Christ in the incarnation could not have been saved by him. In view of developing controversy over the divinity and humanity of Christ, the place of Mary in God's purposes, and the nature of human salvation, the Council of Ephesus was called by Emperor Theodosius II in 431. Cyril attended in order to defend his theological views but the political enmity between him and Nestorius reached fever pitch and Nestorius was hounded as a heretic.

(a) Nestorius

Nestorius was one of the most important figures of the fifth-century Church. His dates are uncertain and all we know is that he was born after 351 and died after 451, but the controversy surrounding him is well known. He was probably born in Germanicia in Syria and spent time in a monastery in Antioch. He soon became widely known as a preacher and speaker. It is probable that he studied under Theodore of Mopsuestia, the 'Nestorian before Nestorius'. Nestorius was, therefore, greatly influenced by the Antiochene approach to theology and its interpretation of Scripture. It is not easy to establish exactly what Nestorius taught and wrote, largely because his written work (sermons and letters) survives only in fragments. Indeed, it has been widely disputed that he actually taught what later became known as Nestorianism and it seems from a work of his known as the *Book of Heracleides*, discovered in the late nineteenth century, that he was at times close to what is now normally thought of as orthodoxy. In any case, he clearly initiated a key debate about Christ in the years between the councils of Constantinople and Ephesus.

In 428 Nestorius was appointed Archbishop of Constantinople by Theodosius II. The power of Constantinople as a see had grown considerably over the years and Nestorius' position as archbishop was therefore very significant. Constantinople was a great imperial see, established as second only to Rome by the Council of Constantinople in 381. It had once been occupied by Bishop John Chrysostom. The Justinian Church of Hagia Sophia was not yet built, but there existed a church built by Constantine's son Constantius.

It seems that early on in Nestorius' episcopate either he or his chaplain Anastasius preached a sermon in which the title Theotokos for the Virgin Mary was partly challenged. Even if the sermon was preached by Anastasius, it was supported by Nestorius and precipitated a controversy that would see Nestorius both condemned and exiled at the Council of Ephesus three years later. Given the strength of the cult of the Virgin Mary, and the popularity of the word Theotokos in Christian worship, any questioning of its legitimacy challenged not only Mary's own status but also that of Christ. For Nestorius and the Antiochenes generally, if Mary was seen as the 'bearer of God', then first, God, who was incarnate in Jesus, had been born; and second, Jesus was divine but not human. Calling Mary 'God-bearer', therefore, undermined the humanity of Jesus and smacked of docetism and Apollinarianism. According to Nestorius, God could not be 'three months old'. He could not undergo change or suffering and could not be born! Jesus himself must have had a real humanity and have undergone growth, change and suffering and it was important to acknowledge this. Nestorius and Constantinople stood as the representatives of the Antiochene tradition in this debate. Not only were they concerned to affirm the humanity of Christ; they wanted to guard the distinction between his divinity and his humanity. They even listed words and deeds of Jesus that showed his divinity in action and those that showed his humanity.

To be fair, it seems that Nestorius' claim was simply that, while the word Theotokos could be used of Mary, it should be supplemented by a number of other titles in order to signal a serious belief in Jesus' true humanity and in the eternal, pre-existent nature of the Father and the Son. Following Theodore, Nestorius suggested that the expressions Anthropotokos ('man-bearer'), Christotokos ('Christ-bearer') and Theodochos ('God-receiver') should be used in order to keep a balance and to mark the belief in Christ's full humanity. Nestorius suggested that the divine and the human were together in 'conjunction' (*sunapheia*) in Christ, rather than in 'union' (*henosis*). This distinction attempted to avoid a 'confusion' of the two natures, as had occurred in the theology of Apollinarius. The differences between these terms was significant and shows how the subtlety of language bore upon the resulting Christology. After asserting the presence of the two natures together in 'conjunction', Nestorius spoke of a unity of *prosopon* or outward appearance. The Greek word *prosopon* meant 'face' or 'external appearance' and indicated that the two natures were united while also remaining inherently distinct. The problem in all this was that for the Alexandrians it looked very much as though Nestorius and his supporters were denying the full divinity of Christ and separating the two natures within him. Before looking at the Alexandrian response to Nestorius it is important to put the debate about Mary in its wider context.

(b) Mary

The place of Mary in early Christian worship and theology forms an important part of the story of how Christ came to be thought of as both divine and human. Mary's importance in the Christian imagination had grown considerably in the centuries before Nestorius and although she does not appear often in the New Testament, the New Testament texts that do refer to her were used frequently by the early Christians. In Paul's letter to the Galatians he says that Jesus was 'born of woman' (Gal. 4.4) but does not say anything about Mary as such. In the Gospels Mary is named with the rest of Jesus' family in Mark 6.3; and, of course, she appears in the infancy narratives of Matthew and Luke (Matthew 1—2; Luke 1—2). She appears twice, unnamed, in St John's Gospel (2.1–5, at the wedding at Cana, and 19.25–27, at the crucifixion). She also appears, named, at the beginning of the Acts of the Apostles (1.14) after the ascension of Jesus. The woman clothed with the sun and with the moon under her feet in Revelation 12 is also often thought to be Mary. Of these texts, the infancy narratives were the ones used most by the early Christians. In fact, Matthew focuses more on Joseph and Luke on Mary, and it is in Luke that the stories of the annunciation (the appearance of the angel Gabriel to Mary), the visitation (the meeting of Mary and Elizabeth), and the presentation (when Mary and Joseph take Jesus to Jerusalem) all occur. In the second century these two infancy narratives were harmonized into another Gospel now known as the *Protevangelium of James*, in which Mary's parents Joachim and Anne also appear. This Gospel is not in the New Testament but was very influential in the centuries that led up to the Council of Ephesus and for many centuries to come.

The main interests in Mary were in her virginity and sinlessness, and in her role in human salvation. She was also seen as an exemplar for Christian behaviour. Early Christians found the idea of Mary's virginity in the Gospels of Matthew and Luke. Matthew uses Isa. 7.14 to bolster his view of Mary's virginity: 'All this took place to fulfil what the Lord had spoken by the prophet: "Behold, a virgin shall conceive and bear a son, and his name shall be called Emmanuel"' (Matt. 1.22–23). The Hebrew of Isa. 7.14

does not use the word 'virgin' (*betulah*) but refers to a 'young woman' (*almah*). However, the Septuagint translation of this is *parthenos*, which means 'virgin'. Matthew clearly sees Mary as a virgin and follows the Septuagint version. In Luke, although Mary is much more prominent, her virginity is perhaps less clear. She is indeed called a virgin at the time of the appearance of Gabriel in Nazareth (Luke 1.27) and it is usually assumed that she remains a virgin throughout the story, although some have claimed that the Holy Spirit comes upon her in the person of Joseph. Matthew says specifically that they did not have sexual intercourse until she had borne a son (Matt. 1.25).

Later discussion of Mary's virginity focused on such matters as whether she was truly a virgin at the time of her conception of Jesus (*virginitas ante partum*); whether she was a virgin at the time of her delivery of Jesus (*virginitas in partu*); and whether she was a virgin after Jesus' birth (*virginitas post partum*). The answers to these questions were mixed and not all were happy to affirm Mary's perpetual virginity. After all, brothers and sisters of Jesus appear in the Gospels and Acts. Those who believed in 'Mary ever-virgin' were reduced to saying that they must have been cousins or children of Joseph by a previous union. In the early second century, Ignatius of Antioch wrote of Mary's role in human salvation, as did Jerome, Augustine and Ambrose (*c.* 339–397) later. Ephraim the Syrian (*c.* 306–373) wrote poetry to Mary affirming her sinlessness. Early on, she was compared to Eve as Jesus was to Adam. As her virginity, sinlessness and importance for salvation were stressed, Mary emerged partly as a somewhat 'docetic' role-model, although she was often also seen as providing a human connection to the increasingly remote Christ. Before the Council of Nicaea, the cult of Mary developed gradually and spasmodically but after that council it flourished.

The debate about whether Mary should be called Theotokos was primarily christological but it took place in the context of the development of all these other ideas about her. The claims that she was the 'bearer of God' and could be called Theotokos, that she had been a virgin, was sinless, and had a key role in salvation, were all interconnected. Now that Mary was so central to Christian doctrine and worship, it is clear why a denial that she was 'bearer of God' could be so threatening to many Christians. In the end, the councils of Ephesus and Chalcedon affirmed Mary as Theotokos: she was the one through whom the eternal Son had been made incarnate in Jesus. Before these councils made their pronouncements, however, there was to be much more debate over Nestorius' views.

(c) Cyril of Alexandria

The main objection to Nestorius came from Cyril, Bishop of Alexandria (d. 444). Cyril was a native of Alexandria and was trained in the Alexandrian methods of theology and scriptural interpretation. He stood firmly in the tradition of Athanasius of Alexandria and of the three Cappadocian Fathers. In 412 he succeeded his uncle Theophilus as Archbishop of Alexandria. Many of his writings survive, including biblical commentaries and sermons, his famous *Paschal Homilies*, and a work against Julian the Apostate, the emperor who tried to reinstate pagan religions over Christianity during his brief reign from 361 to 363. Cyril was a very able and astute theologian but he had a fiery personality and a love of controversy. Soon after his appointment to Alexandria he was caught up in controversy with Jews, pagans and Novatians among others. The story that blackens his character most is the one claiming that he somehow brought about or colluded with the death of the famous Neo-Platonist woman philosopher Hypatia of Alexandria. It seems that if Cyril was not directly responsible for her death, then it was the work of some of his supporters and he did nothing to prevent it. Hypatia was a leading philosopher of her day and was perceived by some as a threat to the Christians in Alexandria because of her support of the Neo-Platonist pagans. Her death was a tragic political affair but it has never been proven that Cyril was actually involved. Whatever the truth about this, the most significant theological conflict in Cyril's life was the one with Nestorius.

Cyril's complaint was twofold. First, in rejecting the use of the word Theotokos for Mary, Nestorius was rejecting the divinity of Christ. The implication was that Jesus was purely human and was no different from other leaders and prophets in Israel's history. Second, Nestorius had failed to assert a real union of the two natures in Christ and had actually ended up separating them. His Christology was therefore dualistic. Although both natures are present in Nestorius' Christ, Cyril claimed, they are not united. And could Christ bring salvation to human beings if his divinity and humanity were not thoroughly united? Therefore, Nestorius, like Apollinarius, was undermining not only the incarnation but also the salvation which was brought to human beings through the incarnation.

When Nestorius became Archbishop of Constantinople, Cyril was immediately provoked to anger over the sermon on Mary as Theotokos. He leapt in quickly to defend the incarnation as he understood it. He affirmed the unity of the two natures in Christ and immediately saw the weaknesses in denying that Mary is the 'God-bearer'. For Cyril, such a claim reduced Christ to a mere man. He accepted that the incarnation consisted of two natures coming together, but wished to affirm 'one nature of the Word enfleshed', that is, once the Word had become enfleshed in Jesus of Nazareth there was only one nature. In fact, Cyril owed this notion to Apollinarius although he thought it came from an orthodox source. In any case, it was this language of 'one nature' that gave Nestorius and his supporters the impression that Cyril was not taking the distinction between the natures seriously: the human nature of Jesus seemed to be simply swallowed up by the divine. In fact, Cyril did speak of a distinction between the natures but rejected the Nestorian word 'conjunction' and always tended to emphasize the union more than the distinction. Cyril's Christology operated on a psychology similar to that of Apollinarius but avoided his errors. Cyril had the notion that the human and the divine natures were continuous with each other and ran into one. He accepted the real humanity of Christ, his limitations in knowledge and his suffering, but he claimed, in brutal paradox, that Christ 'suffered impassibly' on the cross, indicating that he also realized there was a problem in trying to relate the death of Christ to God's eternal changelessness. To top it all, Cyril brought out a connection with the eucharist: he claimed that if Mary was not Theotokos and Christ was only a human being, then the eucharist amounted to cannibalism or eating the flesh of a mere man.

It has become increasingly clear in recent years (not least to some of those Christians who are still separated by these differences) that one of the main points of confusion in the controversy between Cyril and Nestorius was the language each of them used. The meanings of particular words in Greek were different in Constantinople and Alexandria. The key problem was with the word 'nature' (*phusis*). For Cyril 'nature' was a concrete reality, of which there could only be one in the incarnation. To speak of 'two natures' as Nestorius did meant two separate persons, with Jesus like a pantomime horse, manned by two actors though outwardly only one. In the Antiochene tradition, on the other hand, the word 'nature' indicated a less concrete thing and the emphasis on the duality simply affirmed the presence of the two natures united in an external reality. The result of this was that each side perceived the other as saying something more radical than either in fact intended. The theological controversy, fired by intense political wrangling between Constantinople and Alexandria and by the different personalities concerned, soon grew out of all proportion. Nestorius was condemned by a council in Rome in 430. Then John, the Archbishop of Antioch, became involved, along

Historical excursus 5: Ephesus

Ephesus first became famous because of the natural resources of the area in which it was situated. It was a city on the Aegean coast of Asia Minor (modern Turkey) whose geographical position linked it up with the other major cities of the Mediterranean. There are several rivers in the area; Ephesus lay on the River Caister, which emptied into a harbour. The ancient city grew up around various hills in the area and its centre moved several times. Its site was probably inhabited as far back as 1400 BCE but the founding of the city is generally reckoned to have been around 1000 BCE when Greeks were migrating to Ionia. The founder of Ephesus was Androclus.

During this period the first Temple of Artemis was built by the architect Chersiphon. It flourished considerably and made Ephesus famous with the cult of the goddess Artemis. Tradition has it that this temple burned down on the day Alexander the Great was born (356 BCE). After his rise to power the city entered its Hellenistic period, during which the second Temple of Artemis was built under the architect Dinocrates. This temple became one of the seven wonders of the ancient world and made Ephesus world-famous. It burned down in 262 CE and was then rebuilt. This third temple was gradually dismantled by Christians in the fifth century CE.

The city was moved to another location in the same region under Alexander's general Lysimachus in the fourth century BCE. It fell to the Seleucids in the third century and then to the Romans in the first century BCE. It gradually became Christian over the following centuries until it was finally absorbed into the Christian empire after Constantine.

Christian Ephesus begins with the Apostle Paul, who went to Ephesus on his second missionary journey and encountered Demetrius and the silversmiths (Acts 19). The New Testament epistle to the Ephesians was probably not written by Paul and is not specifically directed to Ephesus. It was probably originally a general letter to Christian communities in the area. More important is the fact that Paul wrote at least some of his Corinthian letters from Ephesus (cf. 1 Cor. 16.8). Philippians and Colossians were perhaps also written during the period of Paul's ministry and imprisonment in Ephesus. It is also possible that after Paul's death, Ephesus became a centre of his theology and that his letters were collected there. The non-Pauline Pastoral Epistles (1 and 2 Timothy and Titus) reflect second-century Pauline Christianity, possibly in Ephesus. In any case, there was a Christian community in Ephesus in the second century, to which Ignatius of Antioch wrote a letter. Ephesus is also the setting of Justin Martyr's *Dialogue with Trypho the Jew*. Also in the second century, a tradition stemming from the *Acts of John* (a text recounting the later 'acts' or 'adventures' of the apostle) grew up, claiming that the Apostle John and the Virgin Mary went to Ephesus after the crucifixion of Jesus. The tradition tells of John and Mary living in Ephesus and gathering a community for which John wrote the Gospel and the epistles of John and possibly also the book of Revelation. The traditions concerning John in Ephesus have not on the whole received critical support, but it is clear that Ephesus was a major city in pre-Constantinian Christianity. Its significance to Christians increased after the time of Constantine.

During the Roman period Ephesus was glorified and beautified by a number of emperors. The famous theatre was expanded during the first century CE from its Greek origins to a Graeco-Roman structure seating 25,000. The memorial Library of Celsus was constructed in the second century and housed thousands of scrolls. It was well known throughout the region. The great Arcadian Way was constructed during the reign of Emperor Arcadius (395–408) and ran from the theatre to the harbour. It was a colonnaded street with street lighting like Antioch and Rome. Other features that made Ephesus glorious include temples to various deities and emperors, for example the Temple of Domitian; public buildings of various sorts; baths; aqueducts; fountains; gymnasiums; agoras; and private dwelling places. Most significant from the point of view of the councils is the Church of Mary. There have been several churches on the site, which can be visited today, but although the present remains are later than the Council of Ephesus it seems likely that this was indeed the location of the council. Remains of the later Bishop's Palace can also be seen.

Ephesus was a great centre of learning, culture and art of many different kinds across several hundred years: for instance, the philosopher Heraclitus (d. after 480 BCE) was born there. The city came to be one of the major centres of the ancient Christian world. Indeed, the significance of Ephesus to the Romans was considerable and on four occasions in its history it was granted 'neocorate' status, giving it a special connection to the imperial cult. There is evidence as early as the beginning of the Christian period of the silting up of the harbour, which would gradually bring Ephesus into decline. It seems that the emperors Nero and Hadrian in the first and second centuries were already faced with this problem, though this did not affect sea travel to the city as early as some have claimed. By the time of the Council of Ephesus the harbour was still functioning. By the later sixth century, however, it had thoroughly silted up and Ephesus found itself situated several miles inland from the sea. The glory of Ephesus faded rapidly thereafter.

Today the archaeological site at Ephesus is one of the most impressive in the world. The remains were discovered in the nineteenth century and excavated by John T. Wood and David Hogarth for the British Museum. Wood was looking for the famous Temple of Artemis, which he eventually found, and much more besides. In the twentieth century, excavation was carried out by the Austrian Archaeological Institute of Vienna and today many of the artefacts discovered in Ephesus are housed in the Ephesus Museum in Vienna. There is still much to be uncovered in Ephesus, but we know enough to shed at least some light on what the city was like at the time of the council in 431.

with Theodoret of Cyrus, in order to offer Nestorius support, but matters rapidly got out of hand. Cyril issued twelve anathemas against Nestorius, who responded with twelve anathemas against Cyril (although these are not now thought to have been written by Nestorius himself). Cyril accused Nestorius of separating the natures in the incarnation while Nestorius accused Cyril of confusing them and merging them into one. Both saw human salvation as lying at the heart of the matter. The confusing controversy between Cyril and Nestorius was a significant factor in the build-up that led both to the Council of Ephesus and later to the Council of Chalcedon.

(d) The Council of Ephesus

The Council of Ephesus, called by Emperor Theodosius II, was held in the Church of Mary in June 431 with nearly 200 bishops in attendance. The problem was that the whole affair turned out to be something of a mockery. Cyril and his supporters, including Juvenal of Jerusalem, arrived ready to defend their views. It was arranged that Nestorius would be present with his own supporters from Syria, and that John of Antioch would also be there. In the event, even though Nestorius was in Ephesus at the time of the council he refused to attend and John was delayed because of flooding; and before Pope Celestine's representatives arrived from Rome Cyril decided to open the council, which duly condemned Nestorius. When the full Antiochene party assembled, they called their own council and condemned Cyril! Both parties sought imperial approval and Cyril eventually succeeded in getting the recognition of the emperor in Constantinople. Nestorius was finally condemned and later exiled to Antioch and then (of all places!) Egypt. He was replaced as Archbishop of Constantinople and eventually died in old age, probably in 451, after being generally badly treated.

In addition to condemning Nestorius and affirming Mary as Theotokos the Council of Ephesus produced a series of canons. One of them condemns Pelagianism, the teaching of Pelagius (late fourth to early fifth century) and others, who claimed that human beings can attain their own salvation without divine grace. However, most of the canons concern Nestorius: anyone having anything to do with the Nestorian side of the controversy was deposed; any restorations of deposed Nestorians were invalid; and if anyone had been deposed by Nestorius they were to be reinstated. There were also canons relating to the jurisdiction of bishops

Figure 4 Apse in the 'Council Church' in Ephesus, Turkey. The Council of Ephesus (431 CE) was probably held in an earlier church on this site

saying that they should stay within their provinces. The church in Cyprus was made independent of Antioch.

Although Nestorius had been condemned, Nestorianism survived and was to be condemned again under Justinian at the 'Three Chapters' Council of Constantinople in 553. It persists into modern times in the 'Church of the East' or the 'Assyrian Church of the East', once also known as the 'Nestorian Church of the East'. The Council of Ephesus, then, was rather chaotic but the doctrinal decisions made there marked a turning point in the development of the theology of the councils and Ephesus subsequently became known as the third ecumenical council of the Church.

(e) Conclusion

Even though the Council of Ephesus was a rather muddled series of events it marks an important moment in the development of trinitarian theology and in particular in the emergence of the idea of the divinity and humanity of Christ. Nestorius' reservations about calling Mary Theotokos, which struck many as undermining the divinity of Christ, lost the day at Ephesus and Cyril and his supporters triumphed. The cult of Mary was developing rapidly and by the time of the council it was unthinkable to imply that Mary did not have the status that Christian theology, prayer and worship had begun to give her. As Theotokos, she was now affirmed as the one through whom the eternal Word or Son had been made incarnate in Jesus Christ. In addition, the Antiochene concern to keep the natures of Christ distinct also lost out to Cyril's 'one nature of the incarnate Logos'. Again, it was an issue of salvation, for how could the Nestorian Christ save humanity when his divinity and humanity were so clearly separated? In view of all this, Nestorius' Christology was condemned.

But there was still more controversy to come. Only twenty years separated the Council of Ephesus from the Council of Chalcedon. Although only a short period, those two decades were to be extremely formative for Christian thinking about Christ. After the councils of Constantinople and Ephesus, even though a clearer path was emerging for Christology through the condemnation of Apollinarius and Nestorius, there was still no adequate statement of Christian belief about Christ's divinity and humanity. After each council there were those in every faction who were disappointed with the results, and Ephesus was no exception: it was soon felt that an orthodox christological statement was desperately needed. The question of the most adequate language in which to speak of both the unity of and the distinction between Christ's divinity and humanity, and of the human salvation brought about through Christ, was still every bit as pressing. It would take twenty years and a number of attempts at a formula before further decisions were made on these matters at the Council of Chalcedon in 451.

6

Truly divine and truly human
The Council of Chalcedon (451 CE)

In the summer of 450 Emperor Theodosius II fell from his horse one day while out riding and died. This event was to change the course of history and in particular the course of the councils. After Theodosius' death, his sister, Empress Pulcheria, sought a new consort and Marcian was soon elected emperor. The new emperor expressed a wish to call an ecumenical council of the Church to deal with the ongoing christological controversies and it was arranged that one would be held at Chalcedon, across the Bosphorus from Constantinople, in October 451. This council turned out to be a significant and dramatic event that was later to become known as the fourth ecumenical council of the Church. In terms of Christology it was eventually seen as the most significant of the seven councils, and so of all Church councils. It produced a 'definition' of the relation between the divine and the human in Christ that has both united and divided different groups of Christians ever since. Indeed, it was at this council that Christ was officially proclaimed 'truly divine and truly human' although, as we shall see, this language had been used of him before Chalcedon in the Formula of Union.

In the centuries before Chalcedon there had been a long and tortuous search for a formula that spoke adequately of the relation between the divine and the human in Christ. Trinitarian and christological concerns had intertwined to produce a tangled web of debate and controversy through several hundred years and several councils. The Christologies of both Apollinarius and Nestorius had fallen short in one respect or another and a satisfactory understanding of human salvation in Christ was still needed. The eternal Son, 'true God of true God' as claimed at Nicaea, had become incarnate as a real human being, Jesus of Nazareth, and a fitting form of words was required to express this. But all attempts slid down one of two slippery slopes: they ended up either reducing Christ to an ordinary human being or turning him into some sort of demi-god or angel. Indeed, the spectre of turning Christ into a figure that was neither divine nor human, a semi-divine creature, threatened the debate on all sides. Great care had to be taken, therefore, to find the exact language in which to articulate what Christians experienced and believed about Christ, and indeed at the same time to safeguard the unity of God, for Christianity was a monotheistic faith. The Chalcedonian 'definition of faith' produced at the Council of Chalcedon in 451 is a statement of belief that attempted, among other things, to bring together Antiochene and Alexandrian insights. In fact, however, even though it became the most important conciliar statement about Christ, it caused serious divisions between Christians that have persisted to this day.

(a) After Ephesus

After the Council of Ephesus in 431 there were still serious divisions over Christ's divinity and humanity and the differences looked like deepening. However, there is also a real sense in which some of those involved in the debates wanted to see a resolution to the seemingly endless problems. In spite of his sometimes ferocious personality, Cyril of Alexandria was soon in correspondence with John of Antioch in search of some sort of agreed statement. A form of words decided upon at Ephesus (and probably composed by Theodoret of Cyrus) was sent to Cyril and incorporated by him later into 'Laetentur coeli', his letter to John. In this, Jesus Christ is referred to as 'perfect God and perfect man' or 'truly divine and truly human' (meaning 'complete God and complete man' rather than implying a moral evaluation). Cyril and John both agreed on this form of words in 433 and it later played an important part in the Chalcedonian Definition of 451. The wider statement is known today as the Formula of Union and reads as follows:

> We confess, therefore, our Lord Jesus Christ, the only-begotten Son of God, perfect God and perfect Man, consisting of a rational soul and a body begotten of the Father before the ages as touching his Godhead, the same, in the last days, for us and for our salvation, born of the Virgin Mary, as touching his Manhood; the same of one substance with the Father as touching his Godhead, and of one substance with us as touching his Manhood. For of two natures a union has been made. For this cause we confess one Christ, one Son, one Lord.
>
> In accordance with this sense of the unconfused union, we confess the holy Virgin to be *Theotokos*, because God the Word became incarnate and was made man, and from the very conception united to himself the temple taken from her. And as to the expressions concerning the Lord in the Gospels

and Epistles, we are aware that theologians understand some as common, as relating to one Person, and others they distinguish, as relating to two natures, explaining those that befit the divine nature according to the Godhead of Christ, and those of a humble sort according to his Manhood.

(Stevenson and Frend 1966/1989, pp. 314–15)

The Formula of Union affirms 'two natures' but also stresses union and speaks of 'one person' in addition to using Theotokos of Mary. Cyril seems to have accepted the language of this document and was at least content with its reference to 'two natures'. Also, some of the Antiochenes were ready to accept the word Theotokos for Mary. But there were still many on both sides who were unhappy. In 444 Cyril died and was succeeded in Alexandria by Dioscorus, who carried some of the tendencies of Alexandrian theology to an extreme degree. Flavian was appointed Archbishop of Constantinople and a monk called Eutyches, abbot of a large monastery in Constantinople, became involved in the debate. In short, the major personalities all changed in the years leading up to Chalcedon and a new round of conflict began.

In his Christology, Eutyches (c. 378–454) was an extreme Cyrilline, emphasizing 'one nature' in the incarnation. Whenever the language of 'two natures' was used at this stage it was understood and interpreted by the Alexandrians as being 'before the union': the expression 'out of two natures' was used rather than 'in two natures'. As in Cyril's theology 'nature' (*phusis*) had a more concrete sense for Eutyches, who emphasized the unity. Of course, in claiming that there had been 'two natures' before the union, the Alexandrians were not saying that before the incarnation there had been two separately existing natures; the divinity, the Son, existed separately but the humanity did not. It was simply a manner of speaking to say 'two natures before the union' and 'out of two natures'. In any case, the emphasis was on the 'one nature' of the union. It was obvious to Eutyches that there could only be one nature once the divinity and humanity had come together in Christ. The idea of two 'natures' in the incarnation would have seemed Nestorian. Whatever the exact views of Eutyches, it seems that he took the Alexandrian approach to its logical extreme and held a view of Christ in which the human nature had been completely consumed by the divinity. Once again the humanity of Christ had been undermined through too much emphasis on the divinity and once again there were severe implications for the Christian understanding of salvation.

The situation became more and more politically intricate and Eutyches and his views were condemned at a synod in 448. After this, Flavian of

Historical excursus 6: Chalcedon

Ancient Chalcedon (modern Kadiköy) lies just across the Bosphorus from Istanbul on the Asian side. There have been many theories about the origins of the place name but it may be related to the city of Chalcis in Euboea in Greece. The history of Chalcedon goes back to *c.* 658 BCE, some 17 years before the founding of Byzantium (Greek 'Byzantion'). The area had probably already been inhabited by Phoenicians and Thracians, but then a wave of immigrants from Megara in Greece led by Archias travelled to the Golden Horn area and settled on the plains, choosing it over the area that was later to become Byzantium. The settlers in Chalcedon were called 'blind' because they had not taken advantage of the obviously more strategic and fertile opposite shore. Herodotus, Strabo, Tacitus and Eusebius of Caesarea all tell this story and because of it Chalcedon became known as 'the land of the blind'. Xenocrates, one of Plato's most important disciples, was born in Chalcedon.

During its history, Chalcedon was taken many times in war because of its relative importance in relation to Byzantium. In the fourth century BCE it was captured by the Persians under Darius and then by the Greeks under Philip of Macedon and Alexander the Great. In the first century BCE it was left to the Romans in the will of Nicomedes IV. In the Greek and Roman periods it was known particularly for its Temple of Apollo. In the Roman period it was in the province of Bithynia, like Nicaea. When Constantine the Great made Byzantium his capital in the fourth century CE, he used stone from the ruined Temple of Apollo to build a church on the same site. It was dedicated to the virgin and martyr St Euphemia, who had died in Chalcedon *c.* 303. Later in the same century Emperor Valens took stone from the walls of Chalcedon to build the aqueduct in Constantinople that is still named after him today.

Constantinople decided to appeal to Rome for advice. At this point the second important influence on the Chalcedonian Definition appeared. Pope Leo I, one of the most significant popes of all time and a very able theologian, sent a response to Flavian in the form of a letter containing a lengthy statement of faith. Variously interpreted, the letter has become known as 'Leo's Tome'. Aimed principally against Eutyches and the 'one-nature' party, it has a number of key elements that were to feed into the Christology that was eventually produced at Chalcedon. Leo approached

The cult of St Euphemia of Chalcedon became widely known in the early Christian period. Egeria, the fourth-century traveller from Spain, was aware of it, as were many other Christian writers of the period. Tradition has it that Euphemia was martyred in the early fourth century by burning, beheading or wild beasts. Otherwise, hardly anything is known about her. The church built by Constantine in honour of her was a *martyrion* or 'martyr's shrine' that contained her body. Her remains exuded blood annually and this was distributed to the faithful. Her cult grew to significant proportions. Tradition also has it that Euphemia decided the outcome of the Council of Chalcedon, which was held in the church. The later *Synaxarion of Constantinople* tells us that two texts were put into Euphemia's tomb during the council to see which one she favoured: one Monophysite, the other orthodox. When her tomb was opened several days later to check the result, the orthodox text was in Euphemia's hands while the Monophysite text was under her feet. The Constantinian church in Chalcedon was destroyed in the early seventh century CE by the Persians. The relics of Euphemia were then taken to Constantinople and put into another martyr's church but the iconoclastic emperor Leo III or his son Constantine V had them thrown out. They were soon recovered but were lost when Constantinople fell to the Ottoman Turks under Mehmet II in 1453. Some remains of that church may be found in Constantinople today at the Martyrium of St Euphemia but barely anything is left of ancient Chalcedon. Only a few tombs and a handful of pieces of mosaic are thought to have come from the ancient city and church.

the matter by way of the Trinity, emphasizing that the Son is co-eternal with the Father and that in the incarnation God 'stooped down' to humanity without ceasing to be God. Leo wrote of 'two natures' and 'one person' in the incarnation, stressing that the two natures retain their distinctiveness but act together in one person 'in communion'. Christ performed actions relative to his two natures: the divine nature did divine things while the human nature did human things. The fact that there was 'one person' meant that each nature could be spoken of in terms of the other in a sharing of qualities, interchange of properties or 'communion of idioms' (*communicatio idiomatum*). For Leo, this meant, for example, that one could say that the Son of Man came down from heaven and that the Son of God took flesh from Mary. In this case Leo understands the two titles to refer to Jesus' humanity and divinity respectively. Mary herself is spoken of in the Tome as a virgin, though not as Theotokos. Leo was also at pains to stress that Christ took real human nature from Mary. Overall, the beginnings of a more balanced approach to Christ's divinity and humanity had begun to emerge.

However, by 449 the situation had once again reached such a pitch politically that Theodosius II called another council in Ephesus. This turned out to be an utterly chaotic and unfortunate event. It was dominated by Dioscorus and Eutyches, with the support of Juvenal, Bishop of Jerusalem. Eutyches' views were now reaffirmed, and Leo's Tome, which had been sent to the council, was not even read out. The Antiochene voice was completely silenced by the Alexandrians, who condemned their opponents as Nestorian. Pope Leo later referred to this council as the 'Robber' or Latrocinium (brigandage) Council because the Alexandrians had 'robbed' the Antiochenes and himself of any chance of a hearing. In the face of this it was obvious that another general council would be needed. With the Christology of the Formula of Union and Leo's Tome now circulating, the stage was at least set for the 'two-natures' Christology that would emerge fully at Chalcedon.

(b) The Council of Chalcedon

After Theodosius' disastrous fall from his horse, the new emperor, Marcian, called an ecumenical council for October 451. It was first thought that it might be held in Nicaea, the location of the first council. In the event, the new council was held close to the capital, just across the Bosphorus in the martyr church of St Euphemia in Chalcedon. It began on 8 October and lasted about a month. There were probably about 600 bishops present. There were fifteen sessions, the fifth and sixth of which discussed Christology and produced the famous statement now known as the Chalcedonian Definition. This was signed by 452 bishops at the end of the sixth session. Pope Leo was not present but sent representatives.

The 'definition' that was produced was a detailed statement of faith rather than a definition in the modern sense of the term. It consisted of a statement about the relation between the divinity and the humanity of Christ that all parties in the controversy might agree upon. In fact, it did nothing

Figure 5 The modern Church of St Euphemia in Kadiköy (ancient Chalcedon), Istanbul. The Council of Chalcedon (451 CE) was held in the ancient Church of St Euphemia, probably on this site

to bring christological debate to an end although, apart from those Eastern Christians who rejected it in the years following the council, it was to remain the key statement of faith concerning Christ's natures down to the present time. The Chalcedonian Definition is quite lengthy, incorporating both the Nicene and Constantinopolitan Creeds and standing in full continuity with the Christology of the three previous councils. Indeed, this fourth council affirmed the full significance of the previous three and determined their status as ecumenical. We now turn to the definition itself.

(c) The Chalcedonian Definition

The most important part of the Chalcedonian Definition, concerning the relation between the divine and the human natures in Christ, reads as follows:

> Wherefore, following the holy Fathers, we all with one voice confess our Lord Jesus Christ one and the same Son, the same perfect in Godhead, the same perfect in manhood, truly God and truly man, the same consisting of a reasonable soul and a body, of one substance with the Father as touching the Godhead, the same of one substance with us as touching the manhood, *like us in all things apart from sin*; begotten of the Father before the ages as touching the Godhead, the same in the last days, for us and for our salvation, born from the Virgin Mary, the *Theotokos*, as touching the manhood, one and the same Christ, Son, Lord, Only-begotten, to be acknowledged in two natures, without confusion, without change, without division, without separation; the distinction of natures being in no way abolished because of the union, but rather the characteristic property of each nature being preserved, and concurring into one Person and one subsistence [Greek *hypostasis*], not as if Christ were parted or divided into two persons, but one and the same Son and only-begotten God, Word, Lord, Jesus Christ; even as the Prophets from the beginning spoke concerning him, and our Lord Jesus Christ instructed us, and the Creed of the Fathers has handed down to us.
>
> (Stevenson and Frend 1966/1989, pp. 352–3; italics theirs)

Many commentators have misleadingly interpreted this statement of faith as a mere compromise between the Antiochene and Alexandrian Christologies. For the Antiochenes, it is claimed, there is an emphasis on two distinct natures 'without confusion' and 'without change' and there is due focus on the real humanity of Christ. For the Alexandrians, meanwhile, there is emphasis on one 'person' and one '*hypostasis*', 'without division' and 'without separation', a clear reference to Christ's divinity, and the use of Theotokos for Mary. According to this view, both traditions could find the distinctive emphases of their Christology here. But the definition is far more than just a compromise; it is a finely balanced statement of the complex relation between Christ's divinity and humanity, bringing together elements from both approaches but adding significantly deeper insights into the person of Christ. Unfortunately, the theological and political effects of the definition were to be very divisive indeed. Many Alexandrians perceived it as Nestorian while many Antiochenes perceived it as Eutychian.

The Chalcedonian Definition begins by affirming its continuity with previous councils, that is, Nicaea, Constantinople and Ephesus. The bishops did not want Chalcedon to be perceived as an innovative council making new claims about Christ; it was supremely important to them that the council stood in line with the tradition so far. The definition is, of course, essentially a confession of faith rather than a detached philosophical statement of belief (the Fathers 'confess' its contents) although it is inevitably couched in the language of Greek philosophy. It is riddled with Greek philosophical distinctions and ambiguities that need to be understood if the overall thrust of the Christology is to be appreciated. It includes early Christian language that we considered in Chapter 1 and that became an important part of Christian tradition and belief. Jesus is confessed as Lord, Christ and Son and the main subject of the statement is the precise relation between the divine and human elements in the incarnation. The next claim, as in the Formula of Union, is that Jesus Christ is both 'perfect in Godhead' and 'perfect in manhood' (complete God and complete man). God is fully present in Jesus, and Jesus is really human. The next expressions use another word, 'truly': he is truly God or divine, and truly man or human. Then, clearly laying to rest Apollinarius' idea that there was no human mind in the incarnate Christ, we learn that he has a reasonable or rational soul as well as a body.

Christ is also 'of one substance' (*homoousios*) both with the Father and with humankind. The meaning of *homoousios* has already been discussed in Chapter 3. In the Chalcedonian Definition it is clearly affirmed that there are two elements which are *homoousios*: one, the divine, is 'of one substance' with God, while the other, the human, is 'of one substance' with humanity. The two natures are not, of course, 'of one substance' with each other. Furthermore, in the incarnation, Jesus Christ is without sin. He is really human, and he is different from other human beings only in that he is without sin. The tradition of Jesus' sinlessness had appeared already in the New Testament (Heb. 4.15; 1 Pet. 2.22). There is no elaboration of it here, just the bare statement that it is the case. The real thrust of the claim is that Jesus is one in his relation with God. Perfect humanity after all must be sinless rather than sinful.

The next phrase in the definition retains an ambiguity: Jesus Christ is 'begotten of the Father before the ages as touching the Godhead'. Arius had agreed with this statement, although it appears here in the context of the Son being 'of one substance with God'. 'In the last days' (as the bishops at the council saw the time since the incarnation), he is the same Son who is born of the Virgin Mary. There is no discussion of Mary's virginity, but it is clear that this is part of the accepted tradition. Even more interesting here is the title which Mary receives, Theotokos. In Chapter 5 we saw the significance of this word in the dispute between Cyril and Nestorius. Mary is now affirmed as the 'bearer of God'; she is the one through whom the eternal Word or Son, the only-begotten of the Father, has been made incarnate in Jesus. The Alexandrian use of the term is endorsed.

The second half of the main section of the Chalcedonian Definition makes some very important statements. First, it reiterates some early Christian titles, again familiar to us from the discussion in Chapter 1: Christ, Son and Lord. These titles are now specifically associated with Jesus' divinity and humanity. The additional 'only-begotten' (cf. John 1.14) qualifies sonship and has the anti-Arian sense of 'eternally begotten'. Then comes the language of 'two natures', which has given this Christology its name: the 'two-natures Christology'. There has been some debate regarding the original text of the definition here. Did it say 'in two natures' (*en duo phusesin*) or 'out of two natures' (*ek duo phuseon*)? It is clear that the text that was passed by the council read 'in two natures' and that even though an earlier version had the more obviously Monophysite 'out of two natures' (*ek*: out of two, or into one) this was changed because of pressure from the imperial commissioners, who wanted to please the West. The four crucial phrases which follow are in many ways the pivot of the whole Chalcedonian Christology. The union of the two natures in the incarnation has occurred, it claims, 'without confusion', 'without change', 'without division' and 'without separation'. The first two expressions are Antiochene: there is no confusion and no change in the divine and the human when they join together in the incarnation. The last two expressions are Alexandrian: there is no division and no separation of the two elements when they join together in the incarnation. In other words they are joined together, yet still distinct.

The definition then goes on to spell this out: 'the distinction of natures being in no way abolished because of the union'. In fact the two natures in the incarnation 'concur' into one *prosopon* or 'appearance'. The word *prosopon* usually meant 'external appearance' or 'face' in Greek. This word is related to the Latin *persona*, which also means the outward appearance of something. Even the Antiochenes were happy with the notion of 'one person' in the incarnation. Lest it be thought that this was a somewhat superficial joining, however, the next phrase fills out the meaning of *prosopon* and affirms a deeper union in the *hypostasis* or that which 'stands under' the surface. In many ways this term indicates the crux of the difference between Antiochenes and Alexandrians. The Alexandrians were much happier speaking of one concretely existing entity in Christ, whereas the Antiochenes wanted to emphasize the duality of entities at this point. Hence the word was used in different ways by Antiochenes and Alexandrians. To the first, *hypostasis* meant a substantial element such as divinity or humanity and there were clearly two; to the Alexandrians it meant a concrete individual and there was clearly only one. However, the Chalcedonian Definition aims to assert the unity of Christ here: there are not two 'external appearances' or two 'underlying entities', but one individual reality which is then also called by a number of traditional titles: Son, only-begotten God, Word, Lord and Jesus Christ. Finally, there is the claim that what has been said here stands in line not only with the teaching of the previous councils and Fathers of the Church but also with the teaching of the prophets of Israel and with Jesus Christ himself. The 'Creed of the Fathers' is a final reference to the creeds of the Church. The sense of tradition is very strong here in a Christology that steers a path around all the pitfalls of the previous centuries in making a statement that rejects Arius, Apollinarius, Nestorius and Eutyches. It also attempts a positive statement about who Jesus Christ is.

Thus emerged the 'two-natures Christology' of Chalcedon. It affirmed one *prosopon* and one *hypostasis* in two natures. Although the expression is not used in the Chalcedonian Definition itself this union of two natures in one *hypostasis* later became known as the 'hypostatic union'. Apart from this major statement about Christ which tried to resolve serious christological controversies, the council produced a number of canons relating to disciplinary matters. Before turning to them, however, it is worth noting a key event that took place at the council and that illustrates something of the division the council ended up causing.

(d) Juvenal's about-turn

The event in question concerns Juvenal, Bishop of Jerusalem from *c.* 422 to *c.* 458. He had been at the Council of Ephesus in 431 as well as the 'Robber Council' in 449. An ambitious man, he wanted to raise the status of the Jerusalem diocese in the region. When he took office, Jerusalem fell under the jurisdiction of Caesarea Maritima and ultimately of Antioch in Syria. Juvenal wanted it to be autonomous. Theologically, he was a supporter of the Alexandrians even though he found himself under Antioch. He therefore took pains to establish his independence and that of his diocese. He had supported Cyril of Alexandria at Ephesus and had triumphed with him. Now in 451 he set out for Chalcedon, just as thoroughgoing an Alexandrian. In the years before Chalcedon, Juvenal had rejected Leo's Tome on the grounds that it was too Nestorian. What he did not realize when he went to Chalcedon was that Leo's Tome would play a serious part in the christological definition. The Alexandrian cause was to be balanced by the Antiochene, in that in addition to emphasizing a single 'person' in Christ and using Theotokos of Mary, the expression 'two natures' was to be applied to Christ. Juvenal went into the council at Chalcedon in full support of Dioscorus, Cyril's successor in Alexandria.

However, after the 'Robber Council' the climate had changed. The winds were therefore blowing the other way at Chalcedon, somewhat against the Alexandrian view of Christ, and Dioscorus was deposed at the third session of the council. The threat of losing episcopal status weighed heavily on Juvenal and he immediately made a dramatic about-turn and began supporting the other side! The incident is described in the Acts of the council: Juvenal literally moved from the right side of the church to the left. Although he missed some of the sessions, he took part in the one that, dominated by the general feeling that the Apostle Peter had 'spoken through Leo', eventually accepted the Tome. Perhaps encouraged by the fact that there were still many different views of the definition when it was completed, Juvenal signed it, thereby voting with the victorious party. He had seen the status of Jerusalem raised at Ephesus and it is often claimed that it was at the Council of Chalcedon that it became a patriarchate. This is questionable because the word 'patriarch' meant different things at different times and the formal system of 'patriarchates' only came into existence after Chalcedon. But it does seem clear that at Chalcedon Juvenal's ecclesiastical power and that of Jerusalem increased significantly. Juvenal left the council as a member of the triumphant party, his status as a bishop intact, and the authority of his diocese considerably enhanced.

However, he arrived back in Palestine by boat at Caesarea Maritima to find chaos. An enormous anti-Chalcedonian backlash was splitting his diocese. This took place mostly among the desert monasteries. In fact the only support for Chalcedon was in the monastery of St Euthymius in the Judaean desert. Juvenal was threatened with assassination and returned to Constantinople to seek the emperor's help. In Jerusalem, meanwhile, a new anti-Chalcedonian bishop, Theodosius, was consecrated to take Juvenal's place. The emperor wrote to the monks on Juvenal's behalf, asking them to follow the Chalcedonian faith. As time passed there was movement to and fro: the Empress Eudocia, for example, who had moved to Jerusalem and was supporting the anti-Chalcedonian line, later joined the Chalcedonians. There was much rioting and hundreds of monks were massacred on both sides.

Eventually, after nearly two years, the anti-Chalcedonian Theodosius resigned and Juvenal was able to reclaim his see, albeit with military protection, and return to Jerusalem. But he did not have the full support of the monasteries when he got home. The Christian community was now divided between Chalcedonians and non-Chalcedonians. The problem was that, for many, Chalcedon was a betrayal of the faith of Cyril and the Alexandrians. Juvenal himself was seen as a 'Judas'. But there were also those who thought that Chalcedon was faithful to Cyril and the Alexandrian theology. It was in this climate of conflict that the Chalcedonians separated off from the non-Chalcedonians, later known as the 'Monophysites', that is, those who wished to speak only of 'one nature' after the union of the humanity and the divinity in Christ. The scene was now set for the next stage of the controversy, both in Palestine and in Egypt where the conflict had been even worse.

The incident with Juvenal marked a dramatic turnaround for him personally. In terms of the council itself, it shows that there was still an enormous breadth of interpretation of the language used of Christ in the Chalcedonian Definition and even though the definition was an attempt to bring the different factions together, the controversy was set to continue well into the future.

(e) The canons of Chalcedon

In addition to producing its famous 'definition of faith' the Council of Chalcedon also issued a series of 28 canons. Similar to those of previous councils, and in some instances reaffirming those of Nicaea, they are mostly concerned with ecclesiastical and disciplinary matters. The canons state that:

1 The canons of previous councils are still authoritative.

2 Ordination in return for money is forbidden.

3 Members of the clergy should not work in secular business for money.

4 Monks should not bother themselves with any employment or start new monasteries against the bishop's will.

5 Previous canons about clergy and bishops moving from one place to another shall continue in force.

6 No one is to be ordained without a specific job or church. Those who have been are not to be acknowledged as ordained.

7 Clergy must not take secular employment (cf. canon 3).

8 Clergy should operate under the authority of their bishops.

9 Lawsuits of clergy against clergy should be dealt with internally by the Church and not by secular authorities.

10 Clergy are not to be attached to more than one church.

11 When the poor travel they should have letters of peace from their church but not commendatory letters, which should be limited to those in high regard.

12 No one should try to split ecclesiastical provinces or areas into two.

13 Foreign and unknown clergy must not be allowed to take services without recommendation from their bishops.

14 Readers and singers must not marry women with unorthodox opinions. They must also see that any children are properly baptized into the catholic (orthodox) Church.

15 Women deacons must be over 40 years old and must not marry after they have been ordained.

16 Virgins who have given themselves to God, and monks, must not marry.

17 Country parishes should remain under the authority of their bishops.

18 Clergy should not conspire against their bishop or each other.

19 Bishops in every area are to meet together twice a year.

20 Clergy are not to move over to a church in another city.

21 The character of those who bring charges against clergy and bishops is to be examined by the church.

22 Clergy are not to attempt to take the possessions of a dead bishop.

23 Clergy and monks are not to go to Constantinople and cause unrest.

24 Monasteries are to remain as monasteries once they have been consecrated and must not become secular buildings again.

25 Bishops should be consecrated promptly, and certainly within three months of appointment.

26 Bishops shall have stewards to help manage the affairs of churches.

27 Clergy who take women and pretend to be married shall be depo[...]
    Laity shall be anathematized.
28 Reiterating a canon of the Council of Constantinople, Constantinople,
    the New Rome, is to enjoy a status second only to Rome.

In all these canons further details are provided and recommendations are
made for specific problems, for example individuals might be deposed or
anathematized or a bishop might simply inflict a period of discipline or
exclusion on an individual.

Overall, the canons of Chalcedon give us a vivid sense of the practical
and political concerns that arose alongside the Church's controversies about
the divinity and humanity of Christ. As with the canons of Nicaea and
other councils, they reflect some of the main concerns of the Church of
the day. Clearly there were issues relating to money and work in secular
life as well as authority in the Church. There was a need for order in the
way churches and clergy were organized. There were also still issues relating to orthodoxy and to groups splitting off from what was perceived as
the main body. There were issues relating to married clergy and monks
and obviously relations between the sexes were a key area of concern. Probably the most famous canon from Chalcedon is number 28. It reaffirmed
the importance of Constantinople, which was now second in ecclesiastical
significance only to Rome. The Council of Constantinople had asserted
that its bishop was second only to the Bishop of Rome. At Chalcedon, the
significance of Constantinople in the world of ecclesiastical power was now
further secured. Constantine's city now took its place fully alongside old
Rome.

(f) Conclusion

The Council of Chalcedon marks a significant turning point in the series
of seven ecumenical councils. It was this council that finally proclaimed
Jesus Christ as 'truly divine and truly human'. It produced a christological
statement known as the 'two-natures Christology' which spoke of Christ
as having 'two natures' in 'one person'. In the centuries that followed the
council, the Chalcedonian Definition became the main statement of faith
for many Christians and remains so officially today. But Chalcedon also
gave rise to serious divisions among Christians that have persisted to
this day. Many Christians, especially in the East, rejected the Christology of Chalcedon in the fifth century and continue to do so officially,

)ptic, Syrian, Ethiopian and Armenian churches, among

with the Council of Nicaea, the Council of Chalcedon
and for all the christological controversies with which
produced a statement which tried to avoid the pit-
... too clearly in the theologies of Apollinarius, Nestorius and
Eutyches. The concern at Chalcedon was to stand firm in the tradition;
not to say anything dramatically new; and to produce a form of words
that everyone would find acceptable. However, some Alexandrians continued to be concerned about the language of 'two natures' for Christ and
some Antiochenes reacted against the use of 'one person' for Christ and
of Theotokos for Mary. After the council, of course, the basic theological
agenda was still the same: the wider trinitarian context; the hope of finding the most appropriate language with which to speak about the incarnation; the desire to affirm both the unity of and the distinction between
Christ's divinity and humanity; and the need to speak clearly and adequately
about human salvation. But the various factions involved in the controversy still followed significantly different approaches to these matters.

The picking and choosing from the Chalcedonian Definition on all
sides of the conflict, in combination with the personalities involved and
the political climate of the time, meant that the situation became increasingly explosive after the council. Indeed, Juvenal's behaviour at the
council illustrates just how political the situation had already become.
After Chalcedon numerous factions emerged within the Christian world.
Broadly speaking there were three: those who were relatively content with
the Christology of Chalcedon; those entrenched in a more Antiochene
or Nestorian position, who became known as 'Nestorians'; and those
who became known as 'Monophysites', rejecting the 'two-natures' language of Chalcedon and opting for the 'one-nature' terminology of Cyril,
Dioscorus and Eutyches. Later there were also the 'Neo-Chalcedonians', a
modern term referring to those who reinterpreted Chalcedon in line with
the theology of Cyril of Alexandria in order to convince the Monophysites that Chalcedon was faithful to Cyril's teaching after all. Even within
these groups, views varied enormously and christological language meant
different things to different people. Quite simply, it was a contentious
culture! But the stage was now set for the next wave of controversy, a
controversy that grew out of the 'Monophysite' or 'one-nature' Christology
and eventually became known as 'Monothelitism'.

7

Natures, energies and wills
Two councils of Constantinople
(553 and 680–1 CE)

Even though Christ had been proclaimed as 'truly divine and truly human' at the Council of Chalcedon in 451, controversy over the relation between the two natures and the most appropriate words to express this relation persisted in the centuries that followed. The concern with human salvation and the implications of Christology for the wider understanding of God as Trinity also continued to play a part. There was immediate division in the weeks and months after Chalcedon and the differences between the various groups gradually grew deeper and deeper. In particular, the Monophysite and Nestorian factions became stronger and new tactics were needed to convince them that Chalcedon could be interpreted in a way that would support their views.

The main division in the sixth century was that between the Chalcedonians and the Monophysites. Their disagreement, as we have already seen, was over the question whether Christ had two natures or one. The Council of Chalcedon had affirmed 'two natures' and 'one person' in Christ. The Monophysites, ultimately following Cyril, preferred to speak of 'one nature after the union'. The theological and political drama surrounding this disagreement in the sixth century was largely played out in the cities of Constantinople and Antioch, and involved a colourful and dynamic array of personalities including emperors, patriarchs, popes and many others. Interestingly enough, Antioch now became a stronghold of Monophysitism, especially under its patriarch Severus, one of the chief defenders of the Monophysite cause during this period. He was followed in the same century by the zealous Jacob Baradaeus. A new question also now emerged: if, as Chalcedon claimed, Christ had 'two natures', was it possible that he had only 'one energy' and 'one will'? Some said yes and eventually became known as 'Monenergists' and 'Monothelites'. Others disagreed and affirmed two energies and two wills in Christ after the union. In the seventh century the main supporter of the idea of two wills in Christ was Maximus the Confessor, perhaps the most important of all the Byzantine theologians.

In view of the ongoing christological controversies in the centuries after Chalcedon two further councils were called: one in the sixth century and another in the seventh. Both were held in the capital city of Constantinople, one in 553 and the other in 680–1. The first council, called by Emperor Justinian, dealt with the so-called 'Three Chapters Controversy' and condemned the work of three major Nestorian theologians, among others, in order to appease and encourage the Monophysites. The second council, called by Emperor Constantine IV, dealt with the question of how many energies and wills Christ had and condemned Monenergism and Monothelitism. These two councils of Constantinople have usually been seen as extensions of the Council of Chalcedon, adding nothing substantially new to its Christology. Even so, they became known subsequently as the fifth and sixth ecumenical councils of the Church and are important in their own right.

(a) After Chalcedon

As with the Council of Nicaea in 325, the Council of Chalcedon intensified controversy rather than calmed it. In the West, Pope Leo rejected the twenty-eighth canon of the Council of Chalcedon, which called for a higher status of Constantinople in relation to Rome. There were serious questions of authority at stake and relations between East and West continued to be strained. Leo accepted the Christology of Chalcedon, which was in any case based partly on his own Tome. Throughout the period, theological problems were intertwined with political ambition. We have already seen the split that occurred in Palestine over Juvenal's about-turn and how he arrived back in Palestine to serious riots between Chalcedonians and Monophysites. In Alexandria the situation was also bad. Everywhere, the Monophysites perceived the Chalcedonian Definition as Nestorian and rejected its language of 'two natures': it had been based partly on Leo's Tome and omitted any mention of Cyril's 'one nature of the divine Word'. It spoke of two natures, which for them automatically implied two persons. For those who wanted the emphasis on 'one nature after the union' there was too much emphasis on duality and division and in this the council seemed to have betrayed the fundamental faith of Nicaea.

Of course, the divisions were hardly black and white. Some supported Chalcedon and some rejected it; others changed sides, reconsidered their positions from time to time or sat on the fence. There were extreme Monophysites, who so emphasized unity between the divinity and the humanity in Christ that there was hardly any distinction; moderate Monophysites, who admitted some duality; and Chalcedonians, who followed the 'two-natures' Christology. There were also those, known today as Neo-Chalcedonians, who tried to reconcile Chalcedon with the teaching of Cyril of Alexandria. The Monophysites grew strong, especially in Egypt and Syria, and called those who followed the imperial or Chalcedonian position 'Melkites' ('emperor's men'). There are still Melkite Christians in the Middle East today; and the Egyptian Copts, and the churches in Ethiopia, Syria and Armenia, are still officially Monophysite.

When Emperor Marcian died in 457 he was replaced by a different Leo, who became Emperor Leo I. He supported Chalcedon and sought to unite the various factions in his empire. Anatolius was Patriarch of Constantinople at the time and Peter the Fuller became Patriarch of Antioch. Proterius was Patriarch of Alexandria although the real leaders of the Monophysites in Alexandria were a priest called Timothy Aelurus (the Cat or Weasel!) and Peter Mongus (the Hoarse!). Timothy was later elected Patriarch of Alexandria. For Timothy and Peter, Cyril's 'one-nature' Christology was the only acceptable way forward. But the Chalcedonians were also strong all over the empire. From Constantinople Emperor Leo I wrote to all the bishops of the East asking them what they thought of the Christology of Chalcedon. The response was positive and there was significant rejection of the Monophysite position. As a result, Timothy was exiled to the Black Sea area and replaced by a Chalcedonian, Timothy Salofaciolus (of the white turban or wobble cap!). In 474 Zeno became emperor and, although he was usurped for a year by the anti-Chalcedonian Basiliscus, he was reinstated and decided that he wanted to see unity between the vying Christian factions in the empire. In 482, in conjunction with the new Patriarch of Constantinople, Acacius, and Peter Mongus, Zeno drew up a statement of union that was known as the *Henotikon*, that is the 'instrument of unity' or 'act of union'. The main part of the text runs as follows:

[W]e confess that the Only-begotten Son of God, himself God, who truly took upon himself manhood, our Lord Jesus Christ, who in respect of his Godhead is consubstantial with the Father, and consubstantial with us in respect of his manhood; we confess that he, having come down and been made incarnate of the Holy Spirit and the Virgin Mary, the God-bearer, is one, not two; for we assert that both his miracles and also the sufferings which he, of his own will, endured in the flesh, belong to one single person; we in no wise admit them that make a division or confusion, or bring

111

in a phantom; seeing that his truly sinless incarnation from the God-bearer did not bring about the addition of a Son, for the Holy Trinity existed as a Trinity even when one member, God the Word, became incarnate.

(Bettenson and Maunder 1943/1999, pp. 98–9)

The complete text of the *Henotikon* affirmed the decisions of the first three councils (Nicaea, Constantinople and Ephesus) but did not specifically mention Chalcedon, Leo's Tome or the 'two-natures' Christology. The twelve anathemas of Cyril against Nestorius were affirmed and both Nestorius and Eutyches were condemned. The result of the *Henotikon* was a swift improvement in relations between Constantinople and Alexandria, although differences of perception also quickly emerged. Even though the *Henotikon* was to become the key statement of faith in the Eastern Church during the reign of Zeno it failed to satisfy everyone. In Rome, Pope Felix III rejected it as anti-Chalcedonian and excommunicated Acacius. This led to the so-called 'Acacian Schism' between Rome and Constantinople, which lasted for 35 years from 484 to 519. Different patriarchs in different cities discussed the *Henotikon* over the coming years and conflicting views passed to and fro. Patriarchs and church leaders in the same city often had different views at different times. One significant individual who supported the *Henotikon* was Severus of Antioch.

(b) Severus of Antioch

Severus (*c.* 465–538) is one of the most important Monophysite leaders of the sixth century. He emphasized 'one nature' in Christ in the incarnation and provided the Syrian Monophysites with their main christological concepts and language for centuries to come. Even though he emphasized the divinity of Christ and followed Cyril of Alexandria's emphasis on the unity of Christ's person, he also kept a firm eye on Christ's humanity and for this reason is usually seen as a moderate Monophysite. Severus' contribution to the story of how Christ came to be thought of as both divine and human is considerable not only in terms of his actual theological legacy but also because he spurred the story on into a new phase.

Severus was born in Sozopolis in Pisidia in Asia Minor in 465. He came from a wealthy pagan background and his family were landowners and leaders in their local community. Different accounts of Severus' life have different degrees of reliability but it is possible that his grandfather had been Bishop of Sozopolis and had been among those who had deposed Nestorius at the Council of Ephesus in 431. It is also possible that a group called the 'synousiasts', claiming that in Christ the divine and the human substances were united, was based at Sozopolis. These possibilities may provide some background to Severus' own thought on the divinity and humanity in Christ, for he too was to emphasize unity rather than duality in the relation between the two. When Severus was in his late twenties his father died and his mother sent him and his two elder brothers to Alexandria to study Greek and Latin. His family hoped that he would enter the legal profession and his later writings certainly reflect a legal mind. He also had a keen interest in philosophy, especially that of Libanius. After Alexandria, Severus went to Berytus (Beirut) to study law. While there he was converted to Christianity and began reading the Cappadocian Fathers, who became his theological and spiritual mentors.

Severus was soon attracted to the monastic life and in about 490 entered the monastery of Peter the Iberian in Gaza. At this stage the conflict between the Chalcedonian and the Monophysite monks was raging in Palestine. Severus was quickly caught up in the theological issues regarding the relation between the divinity and the humanity of Christ. He moved to other monasteries in Egypt and eventually founded his own in Maiuma and was ordained. He then spent time in Constantinople as the theological adviser to the emperor. His friendship with other Monophysites such as Philoxenus, Bishop of Mabbug (*c.* 440–523), soon cemented his position as a Monophysite leader. Severus wrote a large number of letters, homilies and other writings that reveal how he responded to the Chalcedonians. His writings also include a formal 'Statement' (*Typos*), which was essentially a Monophysite interpretation of Zeno's *Henotikon*. At one point a controversy over a hymn known as the Trisagion arose. The hymn reads, 'Holy God, holy mighty, holy immortal, have mercy upon us.' The Monophysites added 'who was crucified for us', intending to indicate the unity between the divinity and the humanity in Jesus and thereby deny a Nestorian separation of natures. But the Chalcedonians saw this as 'theopaschitism' – the claim that God the Son, or the Logos, suffered on the cross – and rejected it. The Trisagion reflected a very significant point of difference between Chalcedonian and Monophysite Christology.

As the Monophysite movement gathered momentum Severus became increasingly popular as a theologian and spiritual leader. Eventually, in 512 he was appointed Patriarch of Antioch on the Orontes. Many of his sermons illustrate life in the church and city during this period. It is interesting to see in his sermons a concern with wealth, poverty, corrupt clergy and relations between Christians and Jews in addition to the ongoing controversy about Christology. The conflict between the Chalcedonians and the Monophysites certainly grew deeper during Severus' time as patriarch and he was continually challenged by those who disagreed with him. After six years in office, things turned against Severus when a new emperor, Justin, was appointed in 518. That same year Severus went into exile in Egypt, where he stayed for twenty years until his death. From exile he continued to write in favour of the 'one-nature' Christology and against other views even within his own Monophysite ranks. For example, he was in serious theological disagreement with Julian of Halicarnassus, who believed that Christ's body was 'incorruptible' (*aphthartos*) even before the resurrection. Julian's followers became known as the Aphthartodocetai and flourished particularly in Egypt and Armenia. Severus maintained that it was the resurrection that made Christ's body incorruptible. In 527 Justinian became emperor and soon tried to unite Monophysite and Chalcedonian Christians, but Severus' views had lost popularity. He was eventually accused of Eutychianism (following the views of Eutyches, the extreme Monophysite from the time of the Council of Chalcedon), although by this time most Monophysites had rejected the teaching of Eutyches, and was condemned at a synod in Constantinople in 536. He died in Xoïs (Sakah) near Alexandria in Egypt in 538.

So what exactly did Severus say about the divinity and humanity of Christ? In fact he was far less Eutychian in his Christology than the 536 synod allowed and much more moderate in his emphasis on the unity of the divine and the human in Christ. From a number of works that are still extant it is possible to get a fairly clear picture of his thinking. The main works are: *Against Nephalius* (*Ad Nephalium*); *Against John the Grammarian* (*Contra Impium Grammaticum*); *Against Julian of Halicarnassus* (*Adversus Apologiam Juliani*); and the *Philalethes*, written in opposition to a work that tried to portray Cyril as a supporter of Chalcedonian Christology. As we have seen, for those who disagreed with the decisions and definition of the Council of Chalcedon, talk of 'two natures' in Christ after the incarnation was seriously inadequate. For them it was basically Nestorian in that it separated the natures of Christ. This made human salvation impossible, for if humanity and divinity were not really united in the incarnation there could be no real salvation for human beings. The Alexandrians had always rejected this emphasis on duality or division. In its place, following Cyril, they spoke of 'one nature after the union' of the divine and the human and this is Severus' constant emphasis. He carefully avoids any statements of duality or of two natures in Christ. However, it is interesting to note that in the face of extreme Monophysitism Severus can be found speaking of a duality in human perception and

114

contemplation of the divine and the human in Christ, if not actually in the incarnation itself.

For Severus, the various elements identified in the Chalcedonian Christology, such as 'nature', '*hypostasis*' and 'person', overlap more than his Chalcedonian opponents were prepared to admit. He claims that Chalcedonian Christology involves a contradiction because a single *hypostasis* or person necessitates a single nature: there could not be two natures if there was only one *hypostasis*. The humanity in Christ did not exist independently of the divinity although, of course, the divine Logos had existed from eternity. While Severus always emphasizes unity over duality and division, he is aware of the need to choose the correct language to talk about the relation between the divine and the human. He therefore avoids any language of 'mixing' the divinity and the humanity, maintaining that this leads to a confusion of the elements. He prefers to speak of a 'synthesis' and of a single 'composite nature'.

He also maintains that the incarnate Christ has 'one energy' (Greek *energeia*), by which he means the activity or power of God himself, and 'one will' (Greek *thelema*). These ideas were to become very important in the period following Severus' life and it was out of his thinking that some of the key ideas of the Monenergist and Monothelite theologies gradually emerged. For Severus, the Logos was the governing activity or power in the incarnation: the Logos governed the humanity of Christ in the union. In order to emphasize the role of the divine Logos, Severus speaks of 'theandric energies' (from Greek *theandrike*, 'God-human') when referring to Christ. He sees the notion of Mary as the Theotokos or 'God-bearer' as crucial to Christ's real humanity. He also emphasizes that Jesus' humanity must be seen to be complete if his role as saviour is to be fulfilled. At this point Severus' emphases can perhaps be seen to be pulling in the opposite direction, away from the extreme Monophysite or Eutychian view to a more moderate position.

Severus' christological writings were to influence Syrian theology and spirituality for centuries and he is acknowledged today as one of the greatest of the Syrian theologians. But, as we shall see, the notion that Christ only had only one will was eventually condemned at the Third Council of Constantinople in 680–1.

(c) Jacob Baradaeus

Another important Monophysite figure who gained popularity in the years after Severus' death and who became one of the movement's greatest leaders was Jacob Baradaeus (*c.* 500–*c.* 578). Jacob was Bishop of Edessa in Syria and his Christology and his emphasis on 'one nature' were essentially those of Severus. Jacob was called 'Baradaeus' or 'the man in ragged clothes', apparently on account of the clothes he wore to prevent himself from being recognized by the imperial police, who sought to arrest him for his anti-Chalcedonian activities. During Emperor Justinian's attempts to unify his empire he persecuted the Monophysite Christians and Jacob was often close to arrest but never caught. None of Jacob's writings survives apart from some letters originally written in Greek that have come down to us in Syriac. A great deal of legend surrounds the story of his life and what we know of it is only a skeletal outline, although his significance is beyond doubt in terms of missionary zeal for and the spreading of the 'one-nature' Christology.

Jacob was born on the upper Euphrates near Tella. He became influenced by Monophysite Christianity at an early age and like Severus was attracted to monasticism and the ascetic life. He was educated at a college in Nisibis. In the mid-sixth century, when Ephraim the Patriarch of Antioch was attacking the Monophysites, Justinian's wife, Theodora, who supported them, asked Theodosius, Patriarch of Alexandria, to consecrate a bishop of Edessa in Syria. Jacob was chosen and consecrated *c.* 542 and exercised pastoral responsibility over an enormous area stretching across most of the East. He held office for 36 years in all and influenced Monophysitism in Persia. He certainly proved his mettle as a missionary and, having no fixed abode, travelled constantly across Asia Minor, Armenia, Egypt, Arabia and further afield. He founded churches, consecrated bishops, ordained thousands of priests and spent time in Constantinople under the continuing support of Theodora. He died at Kasion and in 622 his bones were taken back to the area where he was born. Jacob spread the Syrian Monophysite religion and culture across a very wide area. His overall significance for the Syrian Monophysites is indicated by the fact that his followers became known as 'Jacobites' (a name less used by them today).

(d) Justinian and Theodora

Emperor Justinian and his wife Theodora are well known today from a sixth-century mosaic in the Church of San Vitale in Ravenna, Italy, where they can be seen in full imperial dress with their entourage accompanying them. Long before Severus of Antioch died, the young Justinian became influential in the capital as nephew to Emperor Justin I. It was the young Justinian who began the process that was eventually to heal the Acacian Schism in 519. In 527 Justinian became emperor, beginning one of the most significant reigns in the history of Byzantium. He married Theodora, a well-known night-club entertainer, who in her role as empress continued to support the Monophysites. Justinian's reign was largely one of dazzling flamboyance and success. The establishment of the 'new Rome' that had begun with Constantine the Great proceeded apace under Justinian. During his reign, Christianity became even more wealthy and influential and its relations with the state went from strength to strength. Justinian soon embarked upon notable building projects around the empire, including the great Church of Hagia Sophia in Constantinople. There, patriarch and emperor famously joined together in worship symbolizing the unity of Church and state. The liturgy at Hagia Sophia came to symbolize everything truly Byzantine and gave enormous impetus to Church–state relations. Justinian physically transformed Constantinople and built significant structures elsewhere, notably in his Western capital at Ravenna. He also built the Basilica of St John at Ephesus, the monastery of St Catherine in the Sinai desert and the so-called Nea Church in Jerusalem. He rebuilt the Church of the Nativity in Bethlehem. In addition, he formulated his famous 'Code of Justinian', a codification of the laws of the empire that was to have considerable influence on legal systems around the world in later centuries.

During his reign Justinian recaptured parts of the Western empire and brought them under his control. He was generally successful in his attempts to unify the empire, although things were to change later when he lost his grip somewhat and when a plague hit the capital. He was usually able to wipe out anything that stood in his way, closing the famous university in Athens in 529 and limiting the freedom of Jews, Samaritans and so-called heretics and pagans across the empire. He was also largely intolerant of the Monophysites and persecuted them in spite of his wife's continued support of them. Justinian was not only an able administrator and politician; he also took a personal interest in theology. Out of this arose a desire to unite the still-vying factions in the christological debate within the Church. Like many of his predecessors Justinian hoped in this way to unify Christianity. His specific hope was to bring the Monophysites back into the main Chalcedonian fold. In order to achieve this he called several meetings of bishops from both sides of the conflict to discuss christological issues. The Christologies of Eutyches, Cyril and Nestorius, and of three particular Antiochene theologians (Theodore of Mopsuestia, Theodoret of Cyrus and Ibas of Edessa) were debated with varying degrees of success in bringing closer together the parties concerned. Indeed, relations between the various parties continued to deteriorate and Justinian looked for further ways to calm the situation.

In 543 Justinian, in order to give support to the Monophysites, officially condemned some of the work of the three Antiochene theologians. Relations between the East and Rome were now badly strained and the controversy seemed to some Chalcedonians to be taking a decidedly Monophysite turn. Pope Vigilius was particularly concerned at the emperor's condemnation of the Antiochenes and in 548 issued a document called the *Judicatum*, in which he agreed that the theology of Theodore and some of the work of Theodoret and Ibas should be condemned but also reaffirmed the decisions of the Council of Chalcedon. In fact, Vigilius himself oscillated somewhat between Monophysite and Chalcedonian views in the next few years and was never really happy with the outcome of events under Justinian.

By the early 550s it was clear that another council would be needed to address the christological issues and Justinian finally called one in 553. Vigilius was invited to attend and travelled to Constantinople, arriving some time before the council began. He took up residence in the apartment of the papal representative. However, Vigilius had become increasingly unhappy with the direction of christological thinking in Constantinople and felt strongly that he should continue to defend the decisions of Chalcedon, which he thought were being undermined. As preparations for the council were made, relations between Vigilius, the emperor and Eutychius, the Patriarch of Constantinople, grew worse and worse until Vigilius fled across the Bosphorus to the Church of St Euphemia in Chalcedon, where the council had been held in 451, to seek protection. This was a striking physical reaffirmation of the Council of Chalcedon and its decisions. Vigilius refused to attend Justinian's council and only after schism was narrowly avoided did he later give in and support its decisions under pressure from Justinian himself. Eventually, when the council had concluded, Vigilius, now in his nineties, set off back to Rome so exhausted that he died on the way in 555.

(e) The Second Council of Constantinople

Justinian called the council to begin on 5 May 553. It was held in the palace of the patriarch next to Hagia Sophia and was attended by about 165 bishops, mostly from the East, including the patriarchs of Alexandria and

Figure 6 Mosaic of Constantine presenting the city of Constantinople (right) and Justinian the Church of Hagia Sophia (left) to the Virgin Mary, Church of Hagia Sophia, Istanbul. Justinian called the Second Council of Constantinople (553 CE)

Antioch. Eutychius presided over the council. Justinian himself stayed away because he wanted to steer clear of political difficulties.

There were eight sessions, during which a whole range of christological issues was discussed. They focused on the relations between the persons of the Trinity; on the relations between the divine and the human in Christ; and on the status and place of Mary in the incarnation. At the first session a letter from Justinian was read out to the assembly affirming the previous four councils and asking for a consideration of the work of the three Antiochenes. It was at this point that Vigilius, from outside the council, expressed his views in favour of Theodore of Mopsuestia in a statement known as the *Constitutum*. The assembled bishops eventually voted against Theodore and some of the writings of the other two Antiochenes (the so-called 'Three Chapters').

119

Although the council produced no canons as such, 14 anathemas were drawn up. They focused, not on disciplinary matters like the canons of the other councils, but on the central matters of Christology discussed at the council. Most of them dealt with the Christology of Theodore of Mopsuestia, and with some of the work of Theodoret and Ibas. Others anathematized earlier theologians already discussed in other chapters, such as Arius, Apollinarius, Nestorius and Eutyches. Origen's name also appears at the end of the list. The teaching of Origen was outlined in Chapter 2 and his influence was still very much in evidence in the sixth century. Indeed, during the centuries since Origen's death, his theological thinking had formed the basis of a significant system now known as Origenism. Doctrines such as the subordination of the Son and 'universalism' (the belief that all human beings will ultimately be saved), which stemmed from Origen's thinking and were still prevalent but were considered by some to be seriously unacceptable, were condemned. Fifteen other anathemas associated with this council were discovered in 1679. Although they contain material discussed before the council began, they are not part of its original Acts. They condemn various views of Origen and certain beliefs connected with Didymus the Blind, a fourth-century head of the catechetical school in Alexandria and a prolific Alexandrian theologian.

Justinian's council, known today as the Second Council of Constantinople, was only gradually accepted by the Western Church, but it eventually became known as the fifth ecumenical council and was accepted as such by the Third Council of Constantinople in 680–1. By the end of the council in 553, Justinian felt that he had taken a positive step towards unity by condemning some theologians whose theology had been tainted by Nestorian and other views. He had done it primarily to convince the Monophysites that Chalcedon was not as Antiochene as some of them thought, and to draw the various parties together and unite the empire. However, as it turned out he had limited success and the controversy continued. There were still further questions about Christ that had arisen and were causing divisions.

(f) Monenergism and Monothelitism

During the next century there were significant political changes in the Eastern empire in addition to new developments in thinking about Christ. On the political front the rise and growth of Islam began to have serious effects on the eastern borders of the empire and the need to bring the factions within Christianity together became more and more urgent as far as the emperor was concerned. The Persians attacked Jerusalem in 614, taking from the Church of the Resurrection what Christians believed to be the cross on which Christ had been crucified. (It was returned by Emperor Heraclius in 630.) The city fell to Arab Muslims in 638. Chalcedonian and Monophysite groups still vied for power across the empire and the various parties within these groups often did not even agree among themselves. The Monophysites were still dissatisfied with the 'two-natures' language of Chalcedon and wanted to see more emphasis on the unity in Christ. Also, the Second Council of Constantinople had not brought the unity Justinian had hoped for. All of this led the new emperor, Heraclius, to try to unite his empire and, like so many of his predecessors, he felt that if the Christians could be united the empire would be too.

A new focus also now emerged and, as always, philosophical distinctions played their part in the mounting controversy. The point now raised was that if Christ had two natures, as Chalcedon had claimed, perhaps he only had one energy (*energeia*) combining the natures. Furthermore, perhaps he only had one will uniting the divinity and the humanity. Severus of Antioch had already suggested that Christ only had one energy and one will and these ideas were gaining more and more acceptance in some circles. For the Monophysites they were natural developments of the position they already held regarding the unity of the divinity and the humanity in Christ. The notions of 'one energy' and 'one will' also constituted further attempts to negate the Nestorianism that, according to the Monophysites, had prevailed at Chalcedon. 'Nature' was a common enough term by now and, although different people meant different things by it, it was part of the accepted language of Christology. The key question was still whether there was one nature or two.

The word 'energy' had been used by Aristotle to mean 'function', 'operation', 'action' or 'activity' and soon became a very important term in Christian and especially mystical theology. Indeed, its use can already be found in the fourth century, for example in Basil of Caesarea, who distinguishes between the aspect of God that is hidden, his inner nature, and the aspect that is revealed in the world, his 'energy'. It was therefore already a word that had some credibility in the theological vocabulary of the time and indicated an important element within the nature of God. The notion that Christ had 'one energy', therefore, focused on the idea that it was the divine life itself, the energy of God or the divine Logos, that actually energized the humanity in Christ. The sense was of a single active, living power or force motivating and driving the one person. The emphasis was clearly on the unity of Christ and appealed especially to the Monophysites.

Surprisingly, perhaps, some of those from the Nestorian camp also saw advantages in the view that Christ had only one energy, but there was no biblical or patristic support either way for this and a serious controversy soon evolved. Those involved went on to ask whether a single energy in Christ stemmed from the two natures or from his one person. Was the energy rooted in the unity of his person or in the duality of his natures? Those who affirmed one energy became known as Monenergists but others felt that this compromised the Christology of Chalcedon in a Monophysite direction and rejected it outright. After all, talk of 'one energy', especially if that energy were divine, undermined the humanity of Christ and therefore the salvation of humanity.

The controversy rose to such heights that in 638 Emperor Heraclius issued a document known as the *Ekthesis* ('Statement'), probably written by Sergius, Patriarch of Constantinople, and supported at least partly by Pope Honorius in Rome. Although it emphasized the unity in Christ's person it forbade talk of both one energy and two! Instead, it affirmed 'one will' (Monothelitism) and the debate now moved on from the energy itself to its source, the will. How many wills did Christ have? The idea of 'one will' was rather more powerful than that of 'one energy' because the notion of the 'will' raises important questions of intention and morality on the part of the person whose will it is. But if Christ had two wills ('Dyothelitism'), did this not suggest two persons? All this opened a hornet's nest of christological questions and there were at least a couple of biblical texts to consider. For example, should Jesus' prayer in the garden of Gethsemane, 'Abba, Father, all things are possible to thee; remove this cup from me; yet not what I will, but what thou wilt' (Mark 14.36), be interpreted to mean that Jesus had both human and divine wills and thus faced a conflict between the two? Again, in the discourse of the Bread of Life in John's Gospel, Jesus says, 'For I have come down from heaven, not to do my own will, but the will of him who sent me' (John 6.38). This perhaps most clearly indicates a distinction between the will of God and the will of Jesus, which must therefore indicate two wills if Jesus is both divine and human. However, in so far as Christ's will became harmonized with his Father's will, was there not really only one will after all? Such questions about Christ's energies and wills took the christological controversy into a new phase.

In 647/8 Emperor Constans II issued a 'Statement' (the *Typos*) which forbade the assertion of either Monothelitism or Dyothelitism, and ruled that all discussion of Christ should take place within the terms of the first five councils. This statement was intended to follow on from Heraclius' *Ekthesis* and to reaffirm it. As the controversy deepened, however, and as the question of human salvation once again reared its head, various individuals stood up to defend their positions. It was above all Maximus the Confessor who defended the idea that Christ had two wills (affirming his full divinity and his full humanity) and although Maximus eventually died as a result of his views, it was his theology that prevailed at the Third Council of Constantinople in 680–1.

(g) Maximus the Confessor

Maximus the Confessor (*c.* 580–662) is usually regarded as the most important of the Byzantine theologians. Although he is not actually mentioned in the documents of the Third Council of Constantinople, it was essentially his theology that triumphed at that council. It is worth looking at Maximus' theology in some detail, as it illustrates another chapter in the story of how Christ came to be thought of as both divine and human. It shows us what the issues surrounding Monothelitism really were and why the council was called. Maximus has gone down in history as a 'confessor' because of his defence of what later became orthodox teaching concerning the two wills in Christ. Before he died, his tongue was cut out and his right hand cut off for speaking out and writing against the idea that Christ had only one will. This horrific act by those who considered his teaching a threat indicates just how serious the matter was thought to be. Both theological and political issues were raging at this time and a unified empire was as important now as it had been in the fourth century. As before, religious unity was needed in order to undergird political unity in the face of threats from outside. Maximus lived through a tumultuous period.

Reconstructing Maximus' life is not easy as there are conflicting sources. Born around 580 and a member of the upper classes of Constantinople, he was secretary to Emperor Heraclius. In 614 he became a monk at the monastery of Chrysopolis. During the Persian attack on Constantinople in 626 he moved to North Africa, where his encounter with Monothelitism came to a head. He joined a monastery there and soon encountered Sophronius (*c.* 560–638), later Patriarch of Jerusalem. Sophronius may have been abbot of the monastery that Maximus joined but in any case he was an opponent of Monothelitism and influenced Maximus' thinking considerably. Maximus organized several local councils in Africa and took part in the Lateran Council of 649, all of which condemned the Monothelites. Gradually, as he became more widely known, he was asked both to defend his views and to conform to the prevailing Monothelite views. In 653 he was summoned to Constantinople and asked to agree to the *Typos*, which he felt unable to do. He was tried at Constantinople in 655 and, as he also claimed that emperors should have no part in the formation of church dogma, was exiled to Bizya in Thrace. In 661 he was tried again in Constantinople. This time he lost his tongue and right hand and was exiled to Lazica. He died shortly afterwards.

Maximus' theology stands well within the classical Byzantine tradition. Very much an Alexandrian, he followed the Cyrilline interpretation of Chalcedon. His theology is rooted in the Trinity and incarnation and in the monastic tradition of prayer and the spiritual life. The philosophical background to his theology is, of course, Platonism and he struggled with the cosmic theology of the Origenism of his day. He was especially influenced by the writings of such theologians as Evagrius of Pontus (346–399) on the spiritual life; by the Cappadocian Fathers; and by Dionysius the Areopagite (*fl. c.* 500), especially in the way he saw the world as a 'cosmic liturgy' and human life as deification or growing into the likeness of God. For Dionysius the whole of creation existed to worship God and the point of the spiritual life was to get ever closer to God. Maximus' main works include writings on the ascetic life; the *Ambigua*, an exegetical work on Gregory of Nazianzus; the *Mystagogia*, on the eucharist; the *Centuries on Love* and the *Centuries on Theology*; the *Questions to Thalassius*; and the *Opuscula theologia et polemica*. It is the *Opuscula*, especially numbers 3, 6 and 7, that concern the status of Christ's will.

In discussing the questions whether Christ had one or two energies and one or two wills, Maximus went straight to the passage in the Gospels already mentioned, where Christ is praying in the garden of Gethsemane. The key question for Maximus was whether this verse indicates that Christ had one will or two. Obviously Maximus approached the question with a firm belief in the Trinity and in the Christology of Chalcedon: Christ was the incarnate Son consisting of two natures in one person. In fact, in Maximus' discussion of the question how many wills Christ had we see Chalcedonian Christology worked out to the fullest extent yet. Of course, the question of how many wills Christ had also raised questions of what the human 'will' really is in the first place – whether it is free will, and how it relates ultimately to God's will. Because Maximus worked from a basis of Chalcedonian Christology he saw Christ as both divine and human. For him there were, therefore, three elements to be considered: Christ's human will;

his divine will, which is that of the Logos or Son incarnated in him; and the will of God the Father. The question was whether the Gospel verse indicates a case of Christ negating his own human will, 'not what I will', or whether in the process of deciding 'not what I will' he was actually engaged in harmonizing his human will with his divine will and the will of God. It is clear that there are at least two wills here and that is crucial. But Maximus went further, seeing this verse as part of Christ's whole attitude towards death and also as indicating the human capacity to overcome basic human desire. Thus the verse is not just about Christ's wills, but about his whole attitude to his Father and to his human will, desire and passions. For Maximus, the verse indicated the whole process of Christ overcoming sin and passion and embracing God's will.

Equally important as Maximus' emphasis on two wills in Christ is his distinction between the basic will that human beings have by nature, which he calls the 'natural will', and the will which is more commonly thought of as 'opinion', 'inclination' or 'deliberation', which he calls the 'gnomic will' (Greek *gnome*, inclination). Maximus concludes that Christ had two wills largely because he had two natures and therefore logically must have had two wills in order to have been truly divine and truly human. The Chalcedonian logic used by Maximus here is central to his case. The question of salvation is also fundamental once again: if Christ did not have a 'natural' human will, he was not truly human and therefore could not be the saviour of humanity. However, Maximus is equally clear that Christ did not have a human 'gnomic will'. So he was not in constant conflict with himself in having two opinions or in being divided on matters of inclination and decision-making; the natural human will was harmonized with the divine will. For Maximus this is the heart of the Gethsemane prayer and of his argument against Monenergism and Monothelitism. Basically, it is an extension of the Christology of the Council of Chalcedon into the realm of energies and wills.

(h) The Third Council of Constantinople

Maximus the Confessor died before the Third Council of Constantinople was held in 680–1. Monothelite views of Christ had developed even further since his time and as the issues surrounding both Monenergism and Monothelitism raged on, it became clear that another council was needed to deal with the problems. There had been an affirmation of Dyothelitism at a council in Rome under Pope Agatho and now he joined with Emperor Constantine IV Progonatus in calling a council in Constantinople,

Figure 7 The sixth-century Justinian Church of Hagia Sophia, Istanbul. The Third Council of Constantinople (680–1 CE) was held in the imperial palace near here

which began on 7 November 680 and continued until 16 September 681. There were about 174 bishops present and the sessions were held in a hall in the imperial palace known as the Trullos (domed) Hall. There were 18 sessions and the council went on for ten months with long breaks between sessions. It was eventful. The patriarchs of Constantinople and Antioch, George and Macarius, were asked to explain their Monothelitism. During the sessions it was realized that texts from the Fathers of the Church had been misquoted in order to justify their beliefs. George was converted to the two-wills position while Macarius was put on trial and condemned for sticking to one will. A new Patriarch of Antioch, Theophanes, was elected. Another individual, a priest called Polychronius, reckoned he could prove the Monothelite belief by raising a dead man.

A statement of the Monothelite faith was laid on the corpse to no effect and Polychronius was condemned and deposed from the priesthood.

The Third Council of Constantinople produced no disciplinary canons but there were anathematizations of a string of Monothelite leaders including Pope Honorius, who had supported the *Ekthesis* of Heraclius and Sergius in 638. In its various sessions, the council reaffirmed the decisions, Christology and creeds of the five preceding councils, especially that of Chalcedon. It reaffirmed the two natures in the person of Christ and maintained that this pointed to two energies and to two wills. Both Monenergism and Monothelitism were condemned along with those who supported them. The council declared that the letters of Sophronius, Patriarch of Jerusalem, were orthodox in affirming two wills in Christ. Following Maximus the Confessor, it said that although Christ had two distinct wills they were deeply united in the moral sphere, in that his human will was united with God's will. As at Chalcedon, this council affirmed the full unity of Christ in his person or *hypostasis* but not in his natures. Furthermore, the two energies and wills were united, the council claimed, 'without confusion, without change, without division and without separation'. The Chalcedonian Definition, therefore, formed the basis of the Christology of this council and was now restated in support of Christ's two energies and wills. The emphasis on the full divinity and the full humanity of Christ prevailed yet again. After the council a statement of its decisions was hung up at the back of the Church of Hagia Sophia and a letter sent to all the bishops of the empire informing them of the council's decisions against Monenergism and Monothelitism.

(i) Conclusion

The two further councils of Constantinople discussed in this chapter attempted to clear up some of the controversies that arose during the centuries following the Council of Chalcedon. The main question was: did Christ have one nature or two? The Monophysites insisted upon one. The work of Severus of Antioch and of Jacob Baradaeus furthered the Monophysite cause in the East during this period and the 'one nature after the union' argument of Cyril formed the basis of Monophysite Christology. In order to unite his empire, Emperor Justinian sought to draw the increasing numbers of Monophysites back into the Chalcedonian fold. He condemned some of the work of three Nestorian theologians at the 'Three Chapters' council of 553. On the Alexandrian side Origenism was also condemned. These condemnations, however, had little unifying effect and the divisions in the Church continued.

There then emerged the ideas that Christ had one energy or action and one will. These ideas were seen by many to undermine the full divinity and humanity of Christ and therefore to be inadequate in terms of articulating human salvation. The theology of Maximus the Confessor contributed enormously to the detailed working out of Chalcedonian Christology during this period and his theology formed the basis of the Christology of the 680–1 council. Questions of trinitarian theology, language and salvation still permeated the debates and Maximus' contribution certainly underlined the full divinity and the full humanity of Christ. In the end, Chalcedonian Christology and the notion of Christ's two wills prevailed and Monenergism and Monothelitism were condemned at the Third Council of Constantinople.

Even after the two further councils of Constantinople, however, controversy continued and there was reason for a lesser council to be called to reaffirm what had been decided at the two councils. The 'Quinisext Council' ('fifth and sixth' council, so called because it was intended to complete the work of the fifth and sixth ecumenical councils at Constantinople) was called in 692. It was also known as the Trullan Council, as it was held in the Trullos Hall. It was called by Emperor Justinian II and was intended to establish unity in Church and state in addition to reaffirming the two previous councils. The Quinisext Council never became one of the great ecumenical councils of the Church but it did play an important role in reaffirming the councils discussed in this chapter.

After the events of 553 and 680–1 the story of the councils seems to change direction. The subject of debate among Christian theologians at this time seems to move from the question of the divinity and humanity of Christ to that of icons and their use in Christian worship. As we shall see, however, the iconoclastic controversy of the eighth and ninth centuries, far from being a controversy about religious art alone, was at root part of the continuing controversy over Christ's divine and human natures; it was basically a christological controversy and is therefore an important part of the continuing story.

8

Icons and idols
The Second Council of Nicaea (787 CE)

The final chapter in the story of Christ and the seven ecumenical councils concerns a dimension of Christian life and worship that has not appeared so far in this book. That dimension is icons. The story of icons is fascinating and highly significant to the history of the age of the councils. It is not simply a matter of art history or religious and cultural development. It is, in fact, another chapter in the long controversy about the divine and human natures of Christ. The Second Council of Nicaea in 787 decided that icons were a legitimate part of Christian worship and the 'Triumph of Orthodoxy' in 843 reaffirmed this decision. Over the preceding centuries, icon painting (or 'icon writing') had gathered momentum, chiefly in Eastern Christianity. It was a dynamic and extremely powerful form of 'language' in which Christians sought to express and articulate their experience of Christ and of salvation through him. Indeed, icons were seen by some as one of the key ways in which they might 'participate' in the divine life. In any case, they were used increasingly in Christian worship to the extent that some were greatly worried about the part they played. Indeed, by the sixth century serious questions had arisen concerning the very legitimacy of icons. Was their use in worship not tantamount to idolatry and was that not forbidden by one of the Ten Commandments?

In the eighth century Emperor Leo III, the Isaurian, initiated an attack on icons and there followed what was subsequently acknowledged to be the first major phase of iconoclasm. John of Damascus, one of the most famous of the Byzantine theologians of the period, rose up in defence of icons. His *Three Apologies Against Those Who Attack the Divine Images* argued that the incarnation of the Logos in matter legitimized icons. When the Second Council of Nicaea was called in 787 its theological defence of icons was constructed largely from John's theology. However, neither John of Damascus nor the Second Council of Nicaea was able to prevent further iconoclasm. A second major attack on icons blew up under Emperor Leo V in the ninth century. This time Theodore the Studite defended icons from a monastery in Constantinople in his *On the Holy Icons*. Theodore took John's theological defence a step further and rooted his theology of icons more firmly in Chalcedonian Christology. For both John and Theodore a denial of the importance of icons constituted a denial of the incarnation itself. Once again Platonist philosophy and trinitarian theology provided the context of the theological debate and it was claimed that just as the 'other world' was made known in 'this world' in the incarnation, so it was made known through icons. As in previous controversies, the question about icons also bore upon the question of human salvation: how precisely were the divine and the human related in icons and how was God to be worshipped legitimately in the light of them? Before tracing the rise of iconoclasm and the responses of John and Theodore, we must look briefly at the broader background to icons themselves.

(a) Icons and iconoclasm

Human beings have probably always made images of their gods. From time immemorial the Jewish people had asked 'what is God like?' In the narrative of the burning bush, Moses asks for God's name (Exod. 3.14) and at the foot of Mount Sinai the Israelites made and worshipped a golden calf in search of a likeness of God (Exodus 32) and were condemned immediately by Moses. The attraction of images was extremely powerful. But as the Christians were later to discover, there is a thin line between worship and idolatry. In Judaism, images had long been prohibited in the Decalogue or Ten Commandments (Exod. 20.4; Deut. 5.8) although in later centuries the religion was assimilated into a number of different cultures and found itself using images. But the basic fact still stood: God himself could not be portrayed in an image. In the early centuries of the Church, Christians produced many images although there were different attitudes to them. As we shall see, those who argued against icons preserved something of the Jewish attitude that God could not be imaged. Those who argued in their favour, however, claimed that, although God is mysterious and unknowable, he had nevertheless been imaged and made known in his Son Jesus. Indeed, the notion of Jesus as the image of God can be found already in the New Testament (Col. 1.15). In due course, the making of icons, mosaics, statues and frescoes was to become part of Christian worship alongside the more basic images of the cross, the Gospel book and so on.

130

Behind early Christian image-making or 'iconography' stand Egyptian mummy paintings and the portraits on wood discovered in the Nile Valley at Fayyum. Probably the earliest tradition of an image of the face of Jesus is to be found in the Legend of Abgar, which may go back to the fifth century. According to this story, Abgar, King of Edessa, was ill and wrote to Christ for help. Christ did not visit Abgar but sent him an image of his face on a handkerchief or *mandylion*. There is also the tradition, possibly stemming from Theodore the Lector in the sixth century, that St Luke began icon painting with an icon of Mary. This tradition later became very strong and can be found in the writings of St Andrew of Crete and St Germanus of Constantinople in the eighth century. Finally, hard historical fact shows that the earliest known Christian paintings are to be found in the famous catacombs in Rome, the earliest of which date back to the second century. These contain images of, among other things, Christ the Good Shepherd, the Last Supper and the saints. All these examples of 'image-making' have their place in a consideration of the development of icons in early Christianity and it is clear that during the first few centuries Christians made images of Christ, the Virgin Mary and the saints which gradually came to play an important role in their worship.

As the use of icons developed and as their presence in churches became more and more a feature of the Christian liturgical landscape, people began to ask how they should be understood. The Greek word *eikon* simply means 'image' but, as we have seen, images of God had been forbidden in Jewish worship. The question for Christians was now whether images of Christ, Mary or the saints were acceptable to God. As icons became more and more influential, so did the struggle to answer that question. Even more significant, there grew up two main theological responses to icons that were to persist throughout the whole period of the icon controversy in the eighth and ninth centuries. On the one hand there were those for whom icons were perfectly legitimate and who felt that worship was enhanced by their use. For such Christians Christ somehow legitimized the use of images against the Jewish prohibition. Christ had brought in a new dispensation and indeed was himself an 'image' of God. God had also made human beings in his own image (Gen. 1.26) and was himself therefore an 'image-maker'. This surely gave licence to human beings to make images and showed beyond doubt that God could be 'imaged' or made known in an image. These people maintained especially that in the incarnation of the Logos in flesh or matter God himself had shown that he could be imaged in the stuff of creation. On this view, the incarnation legitimized icon-making and use.

On the other hand there were those for whom the presence of icons in worship raised serious questions, especially about idolatry: were not Christians who used icons in worship opening themselves to the possibility of worshipping the images or icons themselves instead of God? Even more importantly, many who held this view argued from the same theological premise as their opponents: if Christ himself was the image of God, as they believed he was and as Scripture claimed, did that not actually preclude the making of further images? If God had made human beings in his image and Christ was an image of God then no further image-making was necessary or desirable: for these Christians, the incarnation rendered any further image-making contrary to the will of God. These two views dominated the theology of icons in the decades before the controversy came to a head.

Those who wished to see icons destroyed because they were idolatrous became known as 'Iconoclasts' or 'icon-breakers'. Those who were in favour of icon-making and use became known as 'iconophiles' or 'lovers of icons', and 'iconodules' or 'venerators of icons'. The two sides were by no means clearly divided and the two positions were by no means clear-cut. In fact, the debate was riddled with many different shades of opinion. There were extreme Iconoclasts not only among the populace but also among rulers and emperors. There were also those with a more moderate dislike of icons who simply wanted them out of general sight in church. Among the extremists there were those who tore down icons from their places in churches and broke them up and burnt them. Almost all the icons across the empire from the period before the iconoclastic controversy were destroyed. However, a few from as early as the sixth century survived under the protection of St Catherine's Monastery in the Sinai desert. This fell under Muslim rule and thus was beyond the reach of the iconoclastic emperors. The icons can still be seen there today.

Among the less extreme reactions to icons was the view that they should be seen as primarily educative. Icons were not so harmful as to require destruction, removal and burning but they needed to be kept at arm's length. They were not to be seen as indicating the real presence of God or of Christ but their subject matter told the story of salvation and they were useful in educating the congregation. The threat of idolatry was reduced if icons played a lesser role in worship. Even those whose attitude towards icons was positive often maintained that they were primarily for purposes of education in the faith, much like the stained glass windows of medieval European churches and cathedrals. For those who were most positive, of course, icons were places where the image of Christ and so of God could be known; they were places of revelation and incarnation. In this mix of views, the accusation of idolatry persisted, however, and iconophiles were accused of worshipping the images on paint and wood, and even worse, of worshipping matter and creation instead of God.

As time passed the accusation of idolatry took root at a serious level and, as noted earlier, resulted in two major waves of iconoclasm. The overall period during which iconoclasm flourished and thousands of icons were destroyed was 725 to 843. A number of factors contributed to the development of iconoclasm: the christological controversy itself; Gnostic and Manichaean views of matter as evil; and the growth of Islam with its prohibition of images, which led some to think that if there were to be conversions from Islam (and indeed from Judaism) Christians had better impose limitations on the use of images. In fact, during the period of iconoclasm the Muslim caliph Yazeed II had many images removed from buildings in his jurisdiction in line with the teaching of the Qur'an. Thus it was that in the first part of the eighth century Emperor Leo III began a campaign against images. In 726 he issued an edict forbidding their use, resulting in the widespread breaking of images and destruction of icons and many other church furnishings. There were those, of course, who ignored the edict and continued to support the use of icons, including Germanus, the Patriarch of Constantinople, who wrote in their favour. The main defender of icons during this period, however, was John of Damascus.

(b) John of Damascus

John of Damascus (*c.* 660–*c.* 750) was probably born in Damascus and worked there in the court of the caliph before moving to Mar Saba monastery near Bethlehem to become a monk. He lived and wrote at a time when Palestine was under the rule of Muslims. Following the life of Muhammad (*c.* 570–632) the new religion of Islam spread rapidly across the Middle East and up to northern Europe including Spain. The Holy Land, including Jerusalem and Bethlehem, was taken in 638 and it was in the following years that the Dome of the Rock and the El Aqsa Mosque were built in Jerusalem. The Islamic context is an important factor in considering John's work, since he operated as a Christian theologian not within the confines of the Christian Byzantine Empire, where iconoclasm was rife, but in the relative protection of the Muslim world, where the climate was very different. While in Islam the prohibition of images was taken very seriously, it was also the case that Muslims rarely interfered with their Christian subjects, so that John's writing in favour of icons near

Bethlehem attracted little attention. John's output was considerable and his thinking came to have a significant influence upon later Christian theology. In the nineteenth century he was acknowledged as one of the 'Doctors of the Church', indicating his perennial importance. John wrote a number of works relating to orthodoxy and heresy and the interpretation of biblical and patristic texts; but our concern here is with his three short works defending the making and use of icons.

During the years 726 to 730 John wrote three works, collectively entitled *Three Apologies Against Those Who Attack the Divine Images*. In these works his theological point of entry into the controversy is creation itself. Indeed, John's entire theology of icons is rooted in a theology of creation. Basically, for John, God is the creator and the creation is good and bears God's stamp. But John does not wish to worship the creation itself. He believes in God the Trinity and maintains that God's Son is the image of God and that God created Adam in God's image. God, therefore, is himself an image-maker. John is aware that the Ten Commandments include a prohibition of images – 'You shall not make for yourself a graven image' (Exod. 20.4) – and he is certainly out to dispel any ideas that icons are idols. He is fully aware of the need to stave off idolatry but is also aware of the need to image God in the world if he is to be known there. The ultimate, incomprehensible God cannot, for John, be 'circumscribed' or captured in an image. But the fact that God is an image-maker and has become united in flesh with humanity in the incarnation makes it possible for an image of the incarnate one to be made. In other words the incarnation, the joining together of divinity and humanity in Christ, has made it possible and even necessary for images of God to be made. Just as the divine and human natures came together in the incarnation, so matter or creation can become united with God in an icon. To deny the legitimacy of icons, for John, is to deny the incarnation itself.

He discusses various types of images and is particularly aware that even though the law of the Jews forbids the making of images, yet their tradition is full of holy physical images: for example, the Tent in the desert, and the Temple of Solomon in Jerusalem and all the furnishings associated with the worship there. Therefore, even though the Law forbade images, it was clear that they could be used in the worship of God. To his Christian opponents who wish to deny the legitimacy of icons on the grounds of Exod. 20.4, John sarcastically asks whether they keep the rest of the Law as well! But there is even more than that. For John, the incarnation has changed what was the case in Judaism. In the incarnation,

God has allowed himself to be imaged in Christ and has therefore given image-making a legitimacy that it lacked before.

John takes this basic theological groundwork further. He is aware that there are questions about how images relate to the things they image. He also responds to the criticism that some Christians are worshipping images. First, he considers how images relate to their 'prototypes' or the things they image, that is Christ, Mary and the saints. The Iconoclasts think that the essence of the image and the essence of the thing imaged is the same and that worshipping with an icon is idolatrous – that is, because God is present in the image and the image is worshipped, the result is idolatry. John, on the contrary, alerts his readers to the subtlety of the icon, for although the honour which is given to an icon in worship is transferred to the prototype – to Christ, Mary or the saints – there is, nevertheless, a difference of essence between the image and the proto- type. After all, the image of the emperor on a coin is in one sense 'the emperor' but it is hardly the emperor himself. John thus shows that the icon is not Christ himself, or Mary or the saints, but is an image or like- ness of them. He continually makes the point that the honour given to an image is transferred to the prototype but the essence of the image is not the same as the essence of the prototype. In many respects the thought here is exactly that which had arisen in Plato's philosophy of Forms and which had permeated Platonism for centuries: the world of shadows is a reflection of the Forms but not the Forms themselves. And icons are a reflection of the divine but not the divine itself.

Furthermore, in the face of the iconoclast criticism that those who use icons are 'worshipping images', John discusses different types of worship. Although the key words overlap in most languages, John makes the basic distinction between 'worship' (*latreia*), which is due to God alone, and 'veneration' (*proskunesis*), which is due to a number of people or things associated with God. In the latter category are Mary and the saints, the holy places in which God became human, for example Nazareth or Bethlehem, and objects associated with worship, such as the Gospel books and crucifixes. Indeed *proskunesis* could be given to the emperor. Another way of putting this is to distinguish between 'absolute worship' and 'relative worship'. Although God alone may be worshipped, the other objects, including icons, may be venerated or adored because the honour given to them passes on to God. The intention of the worshipper in these acts is also an important determinant of how idolatrous the worship is. The bottom line is that John does not wish to worship creation or matter, but the creator who became matter in the incarnation, thus validating the making and use of icons. Finally, John is very concerned to illustrate that the making and use of images is nothing new in his time. At the end of each *Apology* on icons he cites a number of key theologians from the past to show that images have always been used and understood positively. Thus, Basil of Caesarea, John Chrysostom, Ambrose of Milan and Maximus the Confessor are cited frequently.

After John of Damascus had written his three *Apologies*, Leo III's son, Constantine V Copronymos, continued the iconoclastic policies of his father and called a council to ban all icons. The Council of Hieria met in 754 and became known as the 'Iconoclast Council'. It claimed that Christ could not be circumscribed or captured in an image and that all icons should therefore be destroyed. In spite of John's subtle theological response, iconoclasm continued to gather momentum. There were, of course, still iconophiles, who agreed with John's theology and who wished to see his views of icons prevail. Over three decades after the Iconoclast Council another general council was called to address the continuing problem. When Emperor Leo IV came to power, he planned, along with Tarasius, the Patriarch of Constantinople, a council that would reinstate icons. As the controversy flared up again later, the Empress Irene called a council that eventually met in 787. It was largely John of Damascus' theology that was taken up there and used in defence of icons.

(c) The Second Council of Nicaea

The story of the Second Council of Nicaea is particularly dramatic and shows just how fiercely the iconoclasm controversy was still raging at the time the council began. The council opened on 17 August 786 in the Church of the Holy Apostles in Constantinople (rebuilt by Justinian). However, at the first session, Iconoclast soldiers burst into the church and broke up the gathering. It was not to reconvene until over a year later in September 787, this time in the Church of Hagia Sophia in Nicaea (also built by Justinian). Tarasius, Patriarch of Constantinople, presided and about 300 bishops were present. Pope Hadrian I sent two representatives from Rome but the patriarchs of Alexandria, Antioch and Jerusalem were unable to be present because they lived in what was now Islamic territory. The council held eight sessions, the last of which was in the palace of Magnaura in Constantinople with Empress Irene presiding. There are 22 surviving canons which deal with practical and disciplinary matters but the main issue was, of course, the meaning and use of icons. Basically the

Figure 8 The eleventh-century Church of Hagia Sophia, Iznik. The Second Council of Nicaea (787 CE) was probably held in an earlier church on this site

council endorsed the use of icons, adopting the distinction made by John of Damascus between worship (*latreia*), which was to be reserved for God alone, and honour or veneration (*proskunesis*), which could be given to icons. The main section of the council's decree reads as follows:

> Proceeding as it were on the royal road and following the divinely inspired teaching of our holy Fathers, and the tradition of the Catholic Church (for we know that this tradition is of the Holy Spirit which dwells in the Church), we define, with all care and exactitude, that the venerable and holy images are set up in just the same way as the figure of the precious and life-giving cross; painted images, and those in mosaic and those of other suitable material, in the holy churches of God, on holy vessels and vestments, on walls and in pictures, in houses and by the roadsides; images of our Lord and God and Saviour Jesus Christ and of our undefiled Lady, the holy God-bearer, and of the honourable angels, and of all saintly and holy men. For

the more continually these are observed by means of such representations, so much the more will the beholders be aroused to recollect the originals and to long after them, and to pay to the images the tribute of an embrace and a reverence of honour, not to pay to them the actual worship which is according our faith, and which is proper only to the divine nature: but as to the figure of the venerable and life-giving cross, and to the holy Gospels and the other sacred monuments, so to those images to accord the honour of incense and oblation of lights, as it has been the pious custom of antiquity. For the honour paid to the image passes to its original, and he that adores an image adores in it the person depicted thereby.

(Bettenson and Maunder 1943/1999, pp. 102–3)

Thus was sealed the decision of the Second Council of Nicaea concerning icons. But it was not to last long. Like the previous councils, the Second Council of Nicaea did not solve once and for all the issues with which it dealt. It simply sent the debate into a new phase. The council had affirmed that icons could be used in worship and that venerating them was not idolatrous. But after the council, iconoclasm reared its head again, this time under Emperor Leo V, the Armenian. He gained the support of John the Grammarian in preparing for another council to try to rescind the decisions of Nicaea II. In this second period of iconoclasm, Nicephorus of Constantinople, and most significantly Theodore the Studite, spoke out in defence of icons.

(d) Theodore the Studite

Theodore the Studite (759–826) was born in Constantinople and later entered a monastic order in Saccudium in Constantinople where he became abbot. Later still, he moved to Studium, also in the capital city. Theodore wrote a number of texts, including letters, catechisms and hymns, and was caught up in a number of political issues with emperors, not least that concerning icons. He was sent into exile a number of times, most notably by Leo V for defending icons. He followed John of Damascus in his basic theology of icons but developed and extended it in terms of the relation between icons and the incarnation. Theodore's defence was much more christological, focusing on the inner relations between the divine and the human in Christ, and the inner relations between the divine and the material in the icon. Like John before him, he wrote three works *On the Holy Icons*, which are usually read together today. A number of key themes permeate the three pieces and bring the theology of John of Damascus and of the seventh ecumenical council to a christo-logical climax, focusing on the real subject of icons: the incarnation.

At the base of Theodore's theology is, of course, the ultimate incom-prehensible triune God. The key issue, as with John, was whether and to what extent God can be 'circumscribed' or depicted in an image. The answer for Theodore is that God himself cannot be depicted and is thus 'uncircumscribable'. However, the Son, who became incarnate, can be depicted or 'circumscribed' precisely because he became incarnate. As in John's theology, so for Theodore: it was essentially the incarnation that made icons possible although even before that, God had made Adam in his own image and can, therefore, be seen as an image-maker – man him-self is an icon of God! Theodore wrote his works against the Iconoclasts in a dialogue or conversational style which also presents the views of the Iconoclasts themselves. Their main concern is idolatry and Exod. 20.4 is paramount. Here we also have evidence that the Iconoclasts would tolerate icons placed high up in the church so that they could not be venerated or worshipped by the congregation. Theodore's response, again like John's, focuses on the imagery of the Jewish Temple and on Christian use of liturgical aids such as the cross. It is clear from Theodore's text just how complex the debate between Iconoclasts and iconodules had become. They were, of course, agreed about many basic things but the Iconoclasts were concerned to keep true worship for God himself in the narrower sense. Only the consecrated elements of the eucharist, they maintained, were a true image of God and were therefore the only material things worthy of veneration. The real difference between Iconoclasts and icon-odules concerned their understanding of the relationship between the icon and God. Again, the issues were rooted in the philosophy of Plato and Platonism: just as Plato's Forms were reflected in the shadows of this world, so the divine was reflected in matter. Exactly how this relationship was envisaged lay at the heart of the iconoclastic controversy.

It is here, concerning this relationship, that Theodore takes his the-ology further than John and makes specific links between his theology of icons and Chalcedonian Christology. Like John, Theodore uses an illus-tration taken from Basil of Caesarea. Consider a coin with the image of the emperor imprinted upon it. The image is said to be the emperor but there are not two emperors, only one. There is the emperor and his image. And yet we call the image the emperor. Theodore calls the image simply the 'image' and the original, the real emperor, the 'prototype'. They are both alike and yet different. The crucial question is whether the emphasis is to be on the likeness or on the difference. The two elements are the same but different, similar but distinct, and clearly not simply identical. The question, therefore, is 'how alike are they?' Both Iconoclasts and iconophiles spoke of likeness and difference between the image and the thing imaged but the emphases differed. If the emphasis should fall on likeness, the problem of idolatry is greater and the use of icons could result in the worship of the image.

Theodore responds that there is a serious difference in 'essence' (the image is not the emperor himself) but there is also continuity. He deals with this problem in the light of Chalcedonian Christology and draws parallels with the two natures and the one *hypostasis*. In the relation between the icon and its prototype (Christ), he claims, there is a difference in nature (one is Christ while the other is wood) but a continuity and likeness at the level of the *hypostasis* or that which unites. In exactly the same way that in the Chalcedonian Christ the two natures are united in one person or *hypostasis* and yet are also distinct, so the icon is united with its prototype and yet at the same time distinct from it. For Theodore, the question about icons is clearly about the relation between the divine and human natures of Christ, and like John of Damascus he maintains that a denial of the legitimacy of icons is tantamount to a denial of the incarnation itself.

A good deal of the debate and misunderstanding between the Iconoclasts and iconophiles concerned the nature of worship and veneration. The Iconoclasts argued that the words 'icon' and 'idol' really mean the same thing because 'icon' means 'image' and 'idol' means 'form' or 'what is seen'. But Theodore distances himself from pagan idols by saying that idolatry is really committed by those who worship creation and those who do not acknowledge the Trinity. Concerning the veneration of icons, he says that there are degrees of veneration, and following Basil he argues that 'the honor given to the image passes over to the prototype' (Theodore the Studite 1981, p. 57) and is not directed to the material of the icon itself. The Iconoclasts maintained that if, as the iconophiles claimed, there is no similarity of essence between the image and the prototype, there should be no use of icons because one ends up worshipping the material of the icon and, therefore, worshipping the creation. Theodore responds that in as much as there is no continuity of essence between the image and the thing imaged, the veneration of the icon is not of its essence (the physical material of which the icon is made) but of the form of the prototype in the icon, that is, Christ's image. The image of Christ is shown in the icon and is, therefore, worthy of veneration. Indeed, there can be veneration of Christ through the icon because of the unity between them and in spite of the difference of essence. The dominant issue here had to do with degrees of likeness and difference and with degrees of veneration and worship. For Theodore, it is clear that Christ can be venerated through the icon and that the essence of the icon itself is not venerated or worshipped.

Theodore had provided the strongest christological defence of icons to date. But Leo V's iconoclast stance was a force to be reckoned with. A period of political peace ensued and Leo eliminated his iconophile opponents. Theodore the Studite was exiled and Nicephorus the Patriarch removed. John the Grammarian's efforts at producing an iconoclast statement of faith led to a council held in Hagia Sophia in 815. However, in 820 Leo V was assassinated in Hagia Sophia and, although his immediate successors continued his policy, iconoclasm gradually died away. The final chapter in the story is the 'Triumph of Orthodoxy'. In 843, Empress Theodora reaffirmed the use of icons in worship and established the Feast of Orthodoxy, a celebration of the use of icons still held annually in the Orthodox Church on the first Sunday of Lent. A liturgical text in the form of a litany, known as the *Synodicon*, was produced and is still used in the annual celebration. The result of this affirmation of icons both in 787 and in 843 was the continued use of icons in Christian worship and their development as an art form. From the ninth century onwards the use of icons and art generally was to develop and flourish in Christian worship in a wide variety of ways.

(e) The canons of Nicaea II

Like some of the other councils, the Second Council of Nicaea produced a series of canons that are mostly to do with ecclesiastical discipline. There are 22 in all, as follows:

1 The canons of the previous councils are affirmed and the clergy are encouraged to observe them.
2 Anyone becoming a bishop must know Scripture well and the Psalter by heart. Those who do not know Scripture should not be ordained.
3 Any bishop who rises in power through secular channels is to be suspended.
4 A bishop should not make any material profit from those under him.
5 People must not be ordained in return for money.

6 Bishops should gather at least once a year, and the Metropolitan should not take the possessions of other bishops.

7 There should be relics in churches.

8 Jews who only pretend to be Christians should not be encouraged in their pretence.

9 Anyone possessing books against icons should hand them in.

10 Clergy who move to another city without the permission of the bishop should be suspended, and if they have such permission they are not to find secular employment as well.

11 Each church should have its own administrators.

12 Ecclesiastical land should not be handed over to others.

13 Anyone who has handed over church property to outsiders should be suspended from their orders.

14 Anyone performing clerical tasks who is not ordained should cease and desist.

15 Clergy should not hold office in more than one church without permission and certainly not for gain.

16 Bishops and clergy must wear modest dress and not adorn their bodies.

17 No one must attempt to found oratories without proper resources.

18 Women should not live in bishops' houses or in monasteries.

19 People should not be admitted to the clergy or monastic life on the basis of cash payments.

20 There are to be no new 'double monasteries' (i.e. monasteries for both men and women) although the existing ones can continue.

21 Monks and nuns cannot transfer from one monastery to another without permission.

22 Everything must be dedicated to God and eating and drinking must be done in an orderly fashion.

Once again, the canons of a council give us a sense of the range of practical issues that faced the church of the time in addition to the controversies over Christology and icons. There are still issues surrounding money, material profit and authority. Questions of icons (and of relics) are also live issues in this period. In line with this council's chief concern, books against icons are forbidden. Matters of church property seem to be a concern and there are still problems over relations between the sexes and over eating and drinking. Very human issues continued to arise in the Church and with some variations, matters of morality, discipline and authority remained central to the Church's life and concerns.

(f) Conclusion

The Second Council of Nicaea, held in 787, was called to deal with the controversy over the making and use of icons. This controversy was one of the most significant in the history of Christianity. Images of Christ, Mary and the saints had become so popular in Christian worship that there were those who saw their excessive use as idolatrous. There were two main phases of iconoclasm and under two emperors hundreds of icons were broken up and burnt. But the controversy over icons was not just a controversy about religious art. As we have seen, like the trinitarian and christological controversies before it, it was a controversy about the incarnation and about the relation between the divine and human natures in Christ. During the two main phases of iconoclasm John of Damascus and Theodore the Studite, among others, defended icons on the grounds that God himself was an image-maker and that the incarnation legitimized icons. Icons were to be venerated but not worshipped and just as there are two natures in one person in Christ so there are two natures united in one image in the icon. Icons were seen by the iconophiles as places of incarnation and revelation and as thoroughly continuous with God's action in creating human beings and Jesus Christ in his own image. The Second Council of Nicaea affirmed the use and legitimacy of icons. But it did not bring an end to iconoclasm. Further serious attacks were made on icons and only in 843 with the 'Triumph of Orthodoxy' did the making and use of icons finally come to prevail officially in the Church.

It is clear from everything that has been said in this chapter that the same concerns that dominated the previous six councils also dominated the iconoclasm controversy and the Second Council of Nicaea: Christology, language (now the language of icons) and salvation. In the light of this, it is not difficult to see why the Second Council of Nicaea came to be seen as standing firmly in line with the other six councils. In the final chapter we shall discuss the meaning of all seven ecumenical councils for today.

9

The councils today
Positions and prospects

The story of Christ and the seven ecumenical councils of the Church has covered eight centuries of christological development. Those centuries were dynamic and turbulent both politically and theologically, but the ideas about the divinity and humanity of Christ that were thrashed out at the councils and during the controversies surrounding them have remained central to Christianity ever since. After the Second Council of Nicaea in 787 there were no further christological controversies of the sort we have seen in this book. The line of thinking about Christ and the Trinity that emerged from the seven councils has remained in place and has continued to influence Christian theology in both East and West ever since. And the basic idea that Jesus Christ was 'truly divine and truly human' was not to be seriously challenged for many centuries. In the modern and now post-modern periods, however, theologians have finally asked how important some of the traditional ideas about Christ really are and in doing so have challenged the decisions of the ancient councils in new and serious ways.

The concern in this final chapter will be with the place of the councils in Christianity and the various churches today. We shall first briefly retrace our steps in order to underline the real issues that emerged from the seven councils. The concentration on Christ's relation to God, on finding the most appropriate human language to speak about that relation, and on human salvation, will all be underlined. We shall then look at the place of the councils in the major churches today and outline where on a 'map of the councils' some of those churches are to be found. Because some of the ancient divisions caused by the councils are still in place today it will be useful also to discuss some of the ecumenical consultations and dialogues that have occurred in the last half-century or so between some of the separated churches. Some radical changes in approach to Christ during the period of the European Enlightenment will then be outlined in order to illustrate the seriousness of the contemporary challenge to the councils. We shall then draw some conclusions about the possible place of the councils in contemporary Christian theology.

(a) Christology, language and salvation

As we have seen throughout this book, there were at least three major concerns that characterized Christian theological thinking during the period of the councils, all of which emerged in the context of the development of the idea of God as Trinity: first, Christology or the relation between the divine and the human in the person of Christ; second, the most appropriate language to use of that relation; and third, the question of human salvation, widely understood as 'divinization' or participation in the very life of God. It is worth underlining just how these three interests played their part in the story of the councils. The lives of the first Christians had been radically changed by their experience of Jesus. Both Jews and Gentiles saw in Jesus a figure who had revised their basic understanding of their relationship with God and their whole understanding of the purpose of creation. Very early on, probably during Jesus' own ministry, the people who followed him saw him as an extraordinary human being, as somehow more than human, as closely related to God and even as a revelation of God himself. They therefore sought the most appropriate language to evoke and express their vision of him and they used titles and expressions familiar to them from their own religious backgrounds: Lord, Saviour, Son of God, Son of Man and Christ. They went even further and used words and concepts such as 'Wisdom', 'Word', and 'pre-existence' to try to convey their belief that Jesus was fundamentally involved in God's ultimate purposes and was with God even before God began his work of creation, indeed from all eternity.

By the second century there were already differences in emphasis on Jesus' divinity and humanity; by the fourth, controversies were well under way about how he could be both divine and human. Greek philosophical categories and distinctions provided much of the context for the debate. The Council of Nicaea in 325 dealt with the trinitarian controversy over Arius, who claimed that the Son was not co-eternal with the Father. This was rejected as inadequate, especially as far as human salvation was concerned: only God can save; we are saved; Christ brought about our salvation; therefore Christ is divine. As we have seen, the concern with human salvation played an important part in the development of the theology of the councils. After Nicaea, a more specifically christological controversy blew up over the relation between the divine and human natures within

146

Christ. Apollinarius taught that the Logos had taken the place of a human mind in Jesus and was condemned at the Council of Constantinople in 381 on the grounds that if Jesus was not really human he could not really save humanity. The theology of the Holy Spirit thrashed out by the three Cappadocian Fathers was also probably affirmed at this council. In 431 the Council of Ephesus faced two other christological controversies that also bore upon the question of language and upon the Christian notion of salvation. First, Nestorius argued against the use of the word Theotokos or 'God-bearer' for the Virgin Mary. Second, he tried to keep the two natures of Christ firmly distinct from each other. There was intense controversy involving Cyril of Alexandria, and Nestorius was condemned at Ephesus. It is clear that many of the disagreements between these two men arose from their different understandings of some of the theological language they used.

In 451 the Council of Chalcedon made a significant effort to find an adequate form of words that would incorporate both Antiochene and Alexandrian insights. It spoke of Jesus Christ as 'truly divine and truly human' and again the heart of the concern was the theology of salvation. But Chalcedon, with its language of 'two natures in one person', brought much division and disagreement. In the following centuries two further councils were called in Constantinople (in 553 and 680–1) to address the developing non-Chalcedonian Christologies, especially the one which became known as 'Monothelitism' or the notion that Christ had only one will. This had developed in Monophysite circles and again the question of human salvation was uppermost. Throughout all this, Chalcedon remained central to the story in that it provided a yardstick, positive or negative, by which Christians measured each other's Christology.

In the eighth and ninth centuries a new phase in the story was inaugurated in the iconoclasm controversy. Issues concerning the making of icons and their use in Christian worship, linked with the problem of idolatry, brought reactions from John of Damascus and Theodore the Studite. It soon became clear that the fundamental issues were once again the relation between the divinity and humanity of Christ and the salvation of humanity. Another council was called at Nicaea in 787 to deal with the problems. It declared that icons were a legitimate part of Christian life and worship. Even though the iconoclasm controversy was about a different form of 'language' from the other councils, the basic concerns with Christology and salvation were still there.

In the light of the story of Christ and the seven ecumenical councils we must now ask the question 'What is the importance of these councils for Christians today?' Before suggesting how they might form part of an agenda for modern theology we must note that the ancient divisions that emerged at the time of the councils are still very much in place today, especially among the churches of the East. In recent years, however, some of these churches have attempted to overcome some of their ancient divisions through consultation and dialogue. Their main concerns have been the same as those of the councils themselves: Christology, language and salvation.

(b) Churches and councils

Most churches still have councils of some sort and human communities usually make decisions in council. In this sense councils are still important and will probably continue to be so. Whether we think of an international church council such as Vatican II, some sort of national synod, or just a local church council, the basic idea and practice of the council is the same. The situation today concerning the place of the seven ecumenical councils in the Christian churches is primarily that which arose during the period of the councils itself and is reflected in the ecclesiastical divisions that still exist. The Eastern Orthodox churches accept the seven ecumenical councils, which provide the Christology that defines the person of Christ in those churches. The councils also provide the basis and structure of much of these churches' sense of tradition. During the period of the councils itself the individual councils were all seen as related to the previous ones. From the First Council of Constantinople onwards the subsequent councils accepted and reaffirmed their predecessors. The First Council of Constantinople, for example, reaffirmed Nicene orthodoxy and the Council of Chalcedon reaffirmed all the councils that had gone before it and included their creeds in its documents. It was, of course, during the period of the seven councils that the concept of the 'council' gradually developed. The emperor was the one who called them and who often presided over them. The name 'ecumenical' indicated 'the whole inhabited world' of the empire. For the Eastern Orthodox churches, then, the seven councils continue to provide the basis for any continuing theological reflection on Christ and other matters. We may say that these churches set the highest value on unaltering – and unalterable – tradition.

The situation is somewhat different for those churches that do not accept all seven ecumenical councils or that accept more. From the fifth century, as we have seen, some Christians in Palestine, Egypt and the East have not accepted the Council of Chalcedon. Those who believe that it is incorrect and inadequate to speak of 'two natures' in Christ continue to follow the teaching of Cyril of Alexandria and others of that school in referring to 'one nature' in Christ after the incarnation. These churches have become known popularly as the 'Monophysite' churches or more correctly as the 'pre-Chalcedonian' or 'non-Chalcedonian' churches. They include the Coptic Orthodox Church in Egypt; the Ethiopian Orthodox (Tewahedo or 'unionist') Church; the Syrian Orthodox Church; and the Malankara Orthodox Syrian Church in India. The Armenian Orthodox Apostolic Church was not represented at the Council of Chalcedon and subsequently followed these churches in their fundamental rejection of Chalcedonian Christology as they understood it. Strictly speaking, the term 'non-Chalcedonian' also includes the so-called 'Nestorian' Christians of the East (more correctly known as 'the Church of the East' or 'the Assyrian Church of the East'), who reject the councils of Chalcedon and Ephesus (but who are not, of course, Monophysite). They accept only the first two of the seven ecumenical councils and look back to Nestorius, whose ideas were condemned at Ephesus. The Monophysite and Nestorian churches are also known as the Oriental Orthodox churches. They only accept the first three, or two, councils. They exist largely in the East but are increasingly represented in the West, especially in the USA.

The Roman Catholic Church and the churches of the Reformation are in some ways at a very different point on the contemporary 'map of the councils'. The Roman Catholic and Orthodox churches have been divided since the Great Schism of 1054. This break came after centuries of disagreement and tension between East and West and especially between Constantinople and Rome. The origins of the split can be traced back to the beginnings of the councils and were cultural, ideological and political rather than theological. Questions of authority played an enormous part, as did factors that may often seem to be minor differences of custom and ethos. But theological matters such as attitudes to icons and the *filioque* clause (see Chapter 4) also played a role in the final split. From 1054 onwards and especially during the period of the Crusades the churches in the East and the West parted company. The sack of Constantinople by Western Crusaders in 1204 was an outrage which has resounded to the present day. Both continued to hold councils, but while the Greeks now acknowledge the seven discussed in this book as basic, the Latin West (the Roman Catholic Church) now acknowledges 21 as authoritative for its teaching. From time to time there were attempts to reconcile East and West, the high point being the Council of Florence

(1438–45), which was actually attended by both the Emperor of Constantinople and the patriarch, and which reached agreement on virtually all points. But the agreement was rejected once the Greek delegates reported back. The councils in either East or West that followed the seven ecumenical councils did not deal with Christology but were concerned largely with other matters. The last council in the West was the Second Vatican Council of 1962–5. In counting different numbers of councils as authoritative, some churches have had different notions of theological development. Whereas the Eastern Orthodox Churches see the seven councils as fundamental, the Roman Catholic Church, which does acknowledge the pre-eminence of the seven councils, has a broader notion of development through a further 14.

The various so-called 'uniate' churches should also be mentioned here. These are parts of both Chalcedonian and non-Chalcedonian churches that at some point, mostly though not entirely in the seventeenth, eighteenth or nineteenth century, entered into communion with the Roman Catholic Church, retaining their own distinctive traditions but acknowledging the Roman pope as the ultimate authority. On the Chalcedonian side are the Ukrainian Catholic, Greek Catholic (Melkite), Hungarian Catholic and Bulgarian Catholic churches, among others. On the non-Chalcedonian side are the Armenian Catholic, Syrian Catholic and Coptic Catholic churches, among others. These latter certainly acknowledge the first three councils but have so far not formally accepted the last four. There is also the Nestorian Chaldean Catholic Church in Iraq, which is in communion with Rome. All of these churches recognize councils subsequent to the first seven.

The churches of the Reformation, namely the Anglican Communion, the Lutheran churches, and all the churches that arose out of the Reformed tradition, attach greater importance to the first four of the seven ecumenical councils. For example, Article 21 of the Thirty-Nine Articles of the Book of Common Prayer of the Church of England states that councils can in principle be in error. It does not specify which councils are to be acknowledged but the Church of England later unofficially acknowledged the first four. It now maintains that the first four, and especially Chalcedon, contain all the theological beliefs necessary for the salvation of Christians. The sense is that these councils are central to Christian tradition, theology and belief and that they provide the basis (even if not necessarily the final form of words) for Christology. The notion of the development of Christian doctrine and belief, although rooted in the councils, is more open and flexible in the churches of the Reformation than in the Orthodox and Roman Catholic churches. Finally, although the seven ecumenical councils discussed in this book may not be openly or formally acknowledged by some of the free churches that have grown out of the churches of the Reformation, the language of those councils, especially the notion that Jesus was 'truly divine and truly human', permeates their theology and worship, and few Christian groups in the West in the modern period have formally and deliberately rejected any of the seven councils or their Christology.

(c) Ecumenical statements

The churches as they exist today in the East and the West have emerged into their present form as a result of divisions in the fifth century, or of the Great Schism of 1054 and the period of the Crusades, or of the period of the European Reformation. These divisions all remain in place today. In particular, the divisions that emerged in the fifth and sixth centuries after the Council of Chalcedon are still very obvious in the East. But there has been an explosion of dialogue in the last half-century along with various attempts to heal the ancient divisions. In these attempts at unity the participants immediately come face to face with the councils. The debates between the churches involved cast light on the contemporary influence of the councils. Thus, some churches have met together for dialogue and some have produced 'agreed statements' together. In particular, the Orthodox Church has engaged in dialogue with the Oriental Orthodox Churches, and the Oriental Orthodox Churches have engaged in dialogue with the Roman Catholic Church. It is interesting that in their agreed statements the concerns have been predominantly with the main issues that we found in our study of the councils: Christology, language and salvation.

Although there were contacts between the Orthodox and the Oriental Orthodox churches in the early twentieth century, unofficial consultation and dialogue began in earnest in the 1960s under the auspices of the Faith and Order Commission of the otherwise largely Protestant World Council of Churches (WCC). (Perhaps surprisingly, the Eastern churches have all along played a significant part in the WCC while the Roman Catholic Church has stood apart. Eastern Orthodox and Protestant Christians have thus found a kind of common ground!) Four unofficial meetings between the Orthodox and the Oriental Orthodox occurred between 1964 and 1971 and set the scene for more formal dialogue later. These were held in Aarhus in 1964, Bristol in 1967, Geneva in 1970, and Addis Ababa in 1971. These dialogues were held very much in a spirit of respect and of endeavour to find a common thread between the two traditions. The resulting agreed statements stressed the continuing context of belief in God as Trinity, the incarnation, Church, ministry and sacraments, and the common life of the Church. There was a common move against the Christologies of Nestorius and Eutyches and a willingness to see the Christology of Cyril of Alexandria, as commonly understood by both sides, as the way forward. There was a clear emphasis on the centrality of the divinity and humanity of Christ and the Geneva meeting made a distinction between the 'intention' and the 'terminology' of doctrinal formulas, stating clearly that the 'intention' is more important. Indeed, uniformity in actual doctrinal formulas was not seen as necessary at all. In relation to the divinity and humanity in Christ there was an affirmation of the four key expressions from Chalcedon – 'without confusion, without change, without division, without separation' – in order to underline their agreement that there is both a unity and a distinction between the two natures in Christ.

These four unofficial meetings led to the construction of committees that worked on key issues and eventually four more meetings, this time official, were arranged. These were held between 1985 and 1993 as follows: in Chambésy, Switzerland in 1985, St Bishoy Monastery, Wadi Natroun, Egypt in 1989, and Chambésy in 1990 and 1993. Once again the general tone and outcome of these meetings was positive. In the parts of the meetings specifically concerned with Christology there was once again an affirmation of the general context of belief in the Trinity and incarnation; Mary is acknowledged as Theotokos; Jesus Christ is 'truly divine and truly human'; and Nestorianism and Eutychianism, the two extremes that had led to the councils of Ephesus and Chalcedon, are condemned. Also, once again there was a general acceptance of the Christology of Cyril of Alexandria and an acknowledgement of the Oriental Orthodox understanding and use of Cyril's 'one-nature' formula. Again there was a concern to emphasize both the unity and the distinction between the two natures in Christ's person and the four key expressions from Chalcedon were underlined. Both Orthodox and Oriental Orthodox acknowledged that they had three councils in common and that they did not yet both acknowledge the others. But the Oriental Orthodox said they were happy with the theology of icons as laid out at the Second Council of Nicaea in 787, maintaining that their own theology of icons went back well before Nicaea II. There was also an agreement to begin the process of lifting anathemas on the saints of opposing sides. In all this it was generally acknowledged that there is a commonality underneath the ancient christological formulas even though specific terminology had been used in different ways by each side in the past. In these debates and statements, in addition to the obvious christological focus, there is a continuing concern with the role and function of human language in Christology and with the overall implications for human salvation.

We must also note the highly significant developments that have taken place between the Oriental Orthodox churches and the Roman Catholic Church. There have been numerous meetings and dialogues but two Common Declarations come particularly to mind. First, an agreement was signed between Pope Paul VI and Pope Shenouda III of the Coptic Orthodox Church in 1973. This statement includes an affirmation of the perfect divinity and perfect humanity of Christ. The four key expressions from Chalcedon are again used, indicating the strong belief in the unity and also the distinction between Christ's two natures. Mary is acknowledged as Theotokos and Jesus is said to be like us but without sin. Interestingly, there is specific reference to the problem of language, stating that there never can be a fully adequate form of words to speak of the union of the natures in Christ. The statement also rejects Nestorian and Eutychian interpretations of the relation between the two natures of Christ. Second, a Common Declaration was signed between Pope John Paul II and Catholicos Karekin I of the Armenian Orthodox Apostolic Church in 1996. Again, in this statement there is an affirmation of Christ's perfect divinity and humanity and the four key expressions from Chalcedon appear with a view to clinching the crucial unity and distinction between Christ's two natures. This declaration also acknowledges that cultural and political elements in addition to matters of terminology and language have given rise to differences of interpretation and ultimately to division between the churches concerned. Both statements affirm much of the Christology of Chalcedon and acknowledge that much of the misunderstanding over the centuries has been over language.

Finally, we must note relations between the Orthodox and Anglican churches. Formal Anglican–Orthodox dialogue began in 1973 and has resulted in three agreed statements: the Dublin statement of 1974, the Moscow statement of 1976, and the recent Cyprus statement of 2006. In all these, the Trinity, Christology, language and salvation play a central part.

Although there have been numerous other meetings, dialogues and conversations the ones mentioned here have focused on Christology, language and salvation and the prospects for continuing dialogue and possible unity have been generally good. It will be interesting to see what happens at the level of dialogue in the future, both in the Eastern and in the Western churches.

(d) The councils and modern Christology

One final question in this chapter on the councils today concerns what place the councils and their Christology might have in the twenty-first century. To what extent should the councils be authoritative for contemporary Christians? And what is the importance of the notions of the divinity and humanity of Christ for Christians at the present time? The answers to these questions, of course, depend on how we approach the matter. For most Christians today, trinitarian theology still officially provides the context of the belief that Jesus is 'truly divine and truly human', as Chalcedon says. Also, for Orthodox Christians the councils are the backbone of theology and tradition, and the Christology worked out at the councils comprises the content of Orthodox Christian faith. In other churches, as we have seen, the authority of the councils varies. For some Christians only the first two councils are important, for some only the first three, for some only the first four and for others more. For the churches discussed so far in this chapter the significance of the councils is unlikely to decrease in the twenty-first century. Some churches, of course, may begin to acknowledge the significance of more councils in the event of unity and communion with other churches. But there has been little rejection of any of the councils in the modern period. For many Christians, especially in the churches that grew out of the European Reformation, the councils may not seem so central even though historically their churches have acknowledged the first four. Many Christians in the churches in the West are unaware of the importance of the councils of Nicaea or Chalcedon even though these councils have produced the very language with which they worship every Sunday.

An even more difficult question is whether the actual Christology of the seven councils, especially that of Chalcedon, can or should remain central to Christian belief today. Since the European Enlightenment, theologians and philosophers have questioned the relevance of the language of traditional Christology, asking whether it is time to formulate Christian belief in Jesus in new language. For many Christian people in the Western world, especially those unfamiliar with the councils, the idea that Jesus of Nazareth was 'truly divine and truly human' makes little if any sense. There are many reasons, cultural, historical and philosophical, why this is so. The period of the Enlightenment brought radical and substantial changes to the cultures and philosophical mindsets of the people of the period and in post-Reformation Europe there were a number of significant movements that challenged traditional ways of thinking about Jesus. It was in the nineteenth century particularly that the most challenging movements developed, some of them from within Christianity itself. Above all, modern biblical criticism gave rise to a great deal of scepticism regarding the traditional teaching of the Church regarding Jesus. Other significant changes in the philosophical mindset that swept across Europe since the Renaissance, especially the tendency to focus on humanity rather than divinity, gave force to the idea in some quarters that it was simply no longer possible to believe in the divinity of Christ, at any rate in the traditional way. In many ways, modern historical awareness has given rise to the sense that the ideas of the councils have nothing to do with the time of Jesus or with the contemporary Western world.

It was in this climate, largely in Protestant Europe and North America but spreading across the world, that radically new Christologies arose. There were attempts to speak more directly to Christians wherever they were in a language that made more immediate sense to them. The councils were seen to be in need of revision and reinterpretation for a totally different age from the one in which they had originally occurred. Friedrich Schleiermacher in nineteenth-century Germany was one of the first to find serious difficulty with the Christology of Chalcedon. His approach to Jesus was predominantly historical and he claimed that the language of natures and substances as found at Chalcedon simply did not make logical sense. The various 'quests for the historical Jesus' in the nineteenth, twentieth and twenty-first centuries have raised further questions regarding who Jesus was historically, apart from Christian faith in him. Some biblical scholars and theologians have focused simply on Jesus the good man or teacher of morals, others have focused on him as a prophet, while others have seen him as a Spirit-filled agent of God though often simply in the context of his own time. This concentration on Jesus' humanity, especially in Protestant Christianity, has often had the effect of separating the humanity from the divinity and of pushing the divinity out of the picture altogether.

A whole kaleidoscope of Christologies emerged from the middle of the twentieth century onwards including, for example, those from the 'liberation' theologies of South America and the developing world, which relate Jesus to the poor in specific cultures; those in Europe and elsewhere that have attempted to reinterpret traditional Christology through modern philosophical categories such as existentialism; and feminist Christologies that have mostly also abandoned traditional categories altogether. The basic model of Christology as found in the period of the councils has collapsed in some areas although some of the new Christologies were thought by some to stand in line with the traditional approach. In any case, the mainstream churches continue to affirm in their formulas belief in the Trinity, the Christology of the councils, and the language of the divinity and humanity of Christ. In the twenty-first century, in an age of 'postmodernism', philosophical categories have changed again and the wheels are still turning with regard to how to approach traditional Christology. For many scholars today the way to approach Jesus is primarily as a first-century Jew who lived and died during the period of Second Temple Judaism. This approach 'from below', as it has been called, has usually obscured the notion of Jesus being 'truly divine' altogether. For many practising Christians, however, the approach is still 'from above': Jesus is primarily God incarnate, the second person of the Trinity, the eternal Son of God made flesh. This angle emphasizes Jesus' divinity and tends to obscure his humanity.

Thus, even though the traditional Christology of the councils continues to be supported officially by most churches in the modern period, there have been radical challenges to it. Of course, the views of scholars do not necessarily represent official Church belief, but more recently some Christian theologians have rejected the councils altogether or seen them as essentially documents of their own time. Others have concentrated on the divinity or the humanity of Christ, often leaving the two natures to function completely separately. The emphases of ancient Antiochenes and Alexandrians can be seen once again in modern Christologies that emphasize either the humanity or the divinity of Christ. The fact remains, however, that the climate of Christology has changed today and it is hard for many modern Christians not to have a sensitivity to historical change and cultural difference (especially between the first century and later times) that was just not possible in the time of the councils.

(e) Conclusion

Even though the situation in which most Christians live today is radically different from that of the first Christians and even though it may be the case that the Christology of the councils now needs reinterpretation in different cultural and philosophical contexts, some important theological features emerge from the councils that can be useful to contemporary theology. In spite of the radical differences, of course, Christians still in fact use the language of the first Christians and of the councils in their official theology and worship. For instance, Jesus is still very much Lord, Son of God, Saviour and Christ, and frequently pre-existent Word. For most Christians he is still both 'divine and human'. But the real value for Christianity today of the councils and the controversies that surrounded them lies elsewhere.

By way of conclusion I would like to take up the main themes that have emerged during the course of this book. From within the context of trinitarian theology we have noted three main strands in particular. First, there is Christology. The councils invite contemporary Christians to focus seriously on their attitudes to Jesus and to ask the question 'who is Jesus Christ for us today?' Whatever the answer, the councils show how Christians in the early centuries kept the identity of Jesus Christ constantly before them. This focus on Jesus raises the question of his own relation to God and of the relation between the humanity and the divinity within him. These are the main interests of Christology. Christian faith, therefore, ought always to be concerned with Jesus and his relation to God. Second, there is language. The councils show that Christians always need to be aware of the language they use of Jesus' relation to God and of their own relation to Jesus and to God. From the very beginning, Christians sought the most adequate and appropriate language for this and it is clear that the language that is used makes all the difference to what is believed and experienced. Human language is always partly inadequate in theology, as the apophatic tradition in Christianity has stressed, but the task is to find the most appropriate language for any particular context. Third, there is salvation. The councils show that human salvation was one of the main theological issues in the minds of the early Christians throughout the whole period of the councils. The entire story of that period is in a very strong sense the story of Christians trying to articulate their understanding and their sense of their new relationship to God in Christ. Contemporary Christians need to think out their understanding of that relationship too.

In all these areas, of course, the ultimate question is how God or divinity relates to humanity. This is always the central concern of Christian theology and certainly was throughout the age of the councils. The real value of the councils for contemporary Christians can be found not in slavishly following what the Fathers of the councils said simply because they said it, but rather in trying to appreciate more fully what they were trying to do and then doing it after them in our own very different circumstances today. In this sense the agenda provided by the councils is as important today as it ever was in the period of the councils themselves.

The seven ecumenical councils

Council	Date	Issues
Nicaea	325	Arianism
Constantinople	381	The Holy Spirit Apollinarianism
Ephesus	431	Nestorianism The Virgin Mary
Chalcedon	451	Apollinarianism Nestorianism Eutychianism One nature or two in Christ
Constantinople II	553	The 'Three Chapters Controversy'
Constantinople III	680–1	Monenergism Monothelitism
Nicaea II	787	Iconoclasm

Chronology of major figures

Philosophers and theologians	Emperors	Popes
Plato (427–347 BCE)		
Aristotle (384–322 BCE)		
Origen (c. 185–c. 254 CE)		
Arius (c. 260–336)	Constantine the Great (sole emperor 324–337)	Sylvester I (pope 314–335)
Athanasius (c. 296–373)		
Apollinarius of Laodicea (c. 310–c. 390)		
Basil of Caesarea (c. 330–c. 379)		
Gregory of Nazianzus (329/30–389/90)		Damasus (pope 366–384)
Gregory of Nyssa (c. 330–c. 395)	Theodosius I (emperor 379–395)	
Theodore of Mopsuestia (c. 350–428)		
Augustine of Hippo (354–430)		Celestine I (pope 422–432)
Cyril of Alexandria (d. 444)		
Nestorius (b. after 351, d. after 451)	Theodosius II (emperor 408–450)	
Eutyches (c. 378–454)		
Dioscorus of Alexandria (d. 454)	Marcian (emperor 450–457)	Leo I (pope 440–461)
Severus of Antioch (c. 465–538)	Justinian (emperor 527–565)	
Jacob Baradaeus (c. 500–578)		Vigilius (pope 537–555)
Maximus the Confessor (c. 580–662)		(continued overleaf)

Philosophers and theologians	Emperors	Popes
	Constantine IV (emperor 668–685)	Agatho (pope 678–681)
John of Damascus (*c.* 660–*c.* 750)	Irene (empress 780–802; sole empress from 797)	Hadrian I (pope 772–795)
Theodore the Studite (759–826)		

Dates from *The Oxford Dictionary of the Christian Church*, 3rd edn, ed. F. L. Cross and E. A. Livingstone (Oxford: Oxford University Press, 2005).

Glossary

Many of these terms were first used in later periods and would not have
been known at the time. Most of them have a very broad range of
meanings.

adoptionism   the belief that God 'adopted' Jesus during his earthly lifetime and used him for his purposes from that time onwards. This view
often held that Jesus really became 'Son of God' at his baptism.

Alexandrian   a theological tradition associated largely but not entirely
with Alexandria. Its distinctive Christology emphasized 'one nature' in
the incarnate Christ, usually stressing the divine nature more than the
human.

allegory   an interpretation of a narrative or story in which things inside
the text stand for things outside the text.

Anomoeans   extreme Arians of the fourth century, such as Aetius and
Eunomius, who held that the Son was utterly unlike (Greek *anomoios*)
the Father.

Antiochene   a theological tradition associated largely but not entirely with
Antioch. Its distinctive Christology emphasized the distinction between
the two natures in the incarnate Christ, usually stressing the human
nature more than the divine.

Apollinarianism   the teaching of Apollinarius of Laodicea (fourth century) that Christ did not possess a human mind. Condemned at the
Council of Constantinople in 381.

apophatic   of the 'negative way' or *via negativa*, which claims that the
only adequate approach to the knowledge of God proceeds by way of
negative statements. This is contrasted with the 'cataphatic' or 'affirmat-
ive way', which claims that some positive things can be known and said
about God.

Arianism   the teaching of Arius (fourth century) that the Son was *pre-
existent but not co-eternal with the Father. Condemned at the Council
of Nicaea in 325 and again at the Council of Constantinople in 381.
Different types of Arianism prevailed throughout the controversy.

begotten   from 'beget', meaning 'procreate'. The ultimate status of the Son
in his relation to the Father in trinitarian theology. In the Creed of
Nicaea 'begotten not made' contrasts 'begetting' with the more obviously

Arian sense of the Son being 'made' by the Father. In the Niceno-Constantinopolitan Creed the Son is 'begotten of the Father before all the ages'. See also *eternal generation.

canon from Greek *kanon*, 'measuring rod' or 'rule'. (1) An agreed collection of authoritative texts; hence 'biblical canon' means the Bible. (2) A church rule or law, such as the canons produced by the ecumenical councils.

Cappadocian Fathers three eminent fourth-century theologians from Cappadocia: Basil of Caesarea, Gregory of Nazianzus, and Gregory of Nyssa.

Cathari from Greek *katharos*, 'pure'. Another name for followers of *Novatianism, used in the canons of the First Council of Nicaea.

christological from Greek *Christos*, 'Christ', and *logos*, 'word', i.e. 'words about Christ'. Concerning the person of Christ.

Christology the study of the person of Christ, especially the relation between his divinity and humanity.

communicatio idiomatum a Latin expression meaning the 'communion of idioms' or 'interchange of the properties'. The idea that because of the union of the divine and the human in Christ, there is a sharing of qualities between the two natures, and therefore language used of his divinity can also be used of his humanity, and vice versa.

Creed of Nicaea the original creed produced at the Council of Nicaea in 325. This may have been based on a previous creed known to Eusebius of Caesarea or another creed from the Jerusalem church.

Dead Sea Scrolls Jewish documents, including texts of the Hebrew Bible, discovered near the Dead Sea between 1947 and 1956.

docetism from Greek *dokeo*, 'to seem'. The belief that Jesus only seemed to be human and was really purely divine.

Donatists a schismatic body in the African church in the fourth century which refused to accept Caecilian as Bishop of Carthage because, it alleged, Bishop Felix of Aptunga, his consecrator, had been a *traditor*. Donatus, after whom the schism is named, succeeded Caecilian as Bishop of Carthage.

Dynamic Monarchianism an *adoptionist form of *Monarchianism which suggested that the Spirit of God had come to rest upon Jesus during his human life.

Dyophysite from Greek *duo*, 'two', and *phusis*, 'nature'. One who emphasizes the distinction between the two natures of Christ, in contrast to a *Monophysite.

Dyothelite   from Greek *duo*, 'two', and *thelema*, 'will'. One who believes that Christ had two wills rather than one (e.g. Maximus the Confessor), in contrast to a *Monothelite.

Ebionites   from Hebrew *ebionim*, 'poor'. A poverty-stricken group of Jewish Christians in the first century who believed in *adoptionism.

ecclesiology   from Greek *ekklesia*, 'those called out' or 'church', and *logos*, 'word', i.e. 'words about the Church'. Teaching about the Church.

ecumenical   from Greek *oikoumene*, 'of the whole inhabited world', hence 'everyone'. The word was originally used of the councils in the hope that they would involve representatives from everywhere in the Christian world.

edict   an authoritative decree from the emperor, having the force of law.

eternal generation   the doctrine that the Logos or Son of God is 'eternally generated' by the Father, that is, the Son is co-eternal with the Father but the Father is eternally the source of the Son.

Eudoxians   followers of Eudoxius, an extreme *Arian or *Anomoean theologian of the fourth century.

Eunomians   followers of Eunomius, a pupil of Aetius and an extreme *Arian or *Anomoean of the fourth century.

Eutychianism   the extreme *Monophysite view of Eutyches (fifth century) that there was only one nature in the incarnate Christ and that nature was divine. Condemned at the Council of Chalcedon in 451.

filioque   the controversial Latin word meaning 'and the Son', added to the *Niceno-Constantinopolitan Creed in the West in the sixth century, thereby affirming that the Holy Spirit proceeds from the Son as well as the Father.

gnomic will   from Greek *gnome*, 'inclination' or 'opinion'. In the teaching of Maximus the Confessor, this is distinguished from the 'natural will' (a basic volitional capacity). Maximus claimed that, while Christ had a natural human will, he did not have a gnomic will. Christ was not, therefore, divided within himself over basic matters of opinion but did have two wills, one divine and one human.

Gnostic   from the Greek *gnosis*, 'knowledge'. Emphasizing abstract and/or secret knowledge, or 'spiritualizing', underestimating the importance of matter or creation.

heresy   from Greek *hairesis*, originally meaning 'choice' and hence 'sect'. The term gradually came to mean 'theological error' in contrast to *orthodoxy.

Hexapla   Origen's version of the Bible containing six parallel columns of text: the original Hebrew; Hebrew transliterated into Greek; the Septuagint (LXX); and translations into Greek by Aquila, Symmachus and Theodotion.

homoios   Greek, 'like'. Used of the relation between the Son and the Father in the debates surrounding the Council of Nicaea. It was particularly useful because it was ambiguous: the Son was 'like' the Father but also distinct from him.

homoiousios   Greek, 'of like substance', from *homoios, 'like', and *ousia*, 'substance' or 'being'. A word used in opposition to *homoousios in the later Arian debates. *Homoiousios* is vaguer than *homoousios*.

homoousios   Greek, 'of one substance', from *homos*, 'same', and *ousia*, 'substance' or 'being'. The word used at the First Council of Nicaea and in the *Creed of Nicaea to describe the union of Jesus' humanity with general humanity and the union of his divinity with God.

hypostatic union   the union of the divine and human in Christ in the incarnation. The *hypostasis* was that which 'stood underneath' the two natures and formed the unity between the two natures.

icon   from Greek *eikon*, 'image'. An image in paint and wood, used as an aid to prayer.

Iconoclast   from Greek *eikonoklastes*, 'image breaker'. Those who broke up icons or objected to their making and use, especially in the iconoclasm controversy in the eighth and ninth centuries. Iconoclasm was condemned at the Second Council of Nicaea in 787.

iconodule   from Greek *eikon*, 'image', and *douleuo*, 'to serve'. Derogatory *iconoclast term for *iconophiles, characterizing them as those who 'serve' icons.

iconography   from Greek *eikon*, 'image', and *grapho*, 'to write'. The painting of icons.

iconophile   from Greek *eikon*, 'image', and *phileo*, 'to love'. Those who approve of the making and use of icons.

lapsi   Christians who had lapsed in their faith during one of the imperial persecutions. See also *traditor*.

latreia   Greek, 'worship'. The term used by John of Damascus and those at the Second Council of Nicaea to indicate reverence that was due only to God, as distinct from *proskunesis*, honour or veneration that was due to the saints.

Macedonians   a group of *Spirit fighters or *Pneumatomachoi named after Macedonius (fourth century). They denied the divinity of the Holy Spirit and were condemned at the Council of Constantinople in 381.

Manichaeism   followers of the teaching of Mani, Manes or Manichaeus in the third century. An extremely dualistic, *Gnostic philosophy that asserted the existence of two ultimate realities in the universe, good and evil.

Marcellians   followers of Marcellus of Ancyra (fourth century), who taught a version of *Modalism and against whose teaching the phrase 'whose kingdom shall have no end' was inserted into the *Niceno-Constantinopolitan Creed.

mihrab   the semi-circular niche in the wall of a mosque indicating the direction of Mecca.

minaret   the tower on a mosque from which the muezzin chants the 'call to prayer'.

Modalism   the belief that God is ultimately one, and the Son and the Spirit are mere 'modes' of his existence in relation to his creating, redeeming and sanctifying powers. Also called 'Modalistic *Monarchianism'.

Monarchianism   a monotheistic belief that God is ultimately only one. It merges the Son and the Spirit into the Father, stressing the union more than the distinctions in the Trinity.

Monenergism   from Greek *monos*, 'one', and *energeia*, 'energy'. The claim that the incarnate Christ had only one 'energy' or 'action'. Condemned at the Third Council of Constantinople in 680–1.

Monophysite   from Greek *mono*, 'one', and *phusis*, 'nature'. One who claims that there was only one nature in Christ after the incarnation. The word is often used of Armenian, Syrian, Coptic and Ethiopian Christians today, though they themselves reject it, preferring to be called *'non-Chalcedonian' or 'pre-Chalcedonian'. The Council of Chalcedon affirmed 'two natures' in Christ.

Monothelitism   from Greek *monos*, 'one', and *thelema*, 'will'. The claim that the incarnate Christ had only one will. Condemned at the Third Council of Constantinople in 680–1.

Nestorianism   the alleged teaching of Nestorius (fifth century), who supposedly separated the two natures of Christ. The 'Church of the East', associated with Nestorius' teachings down the centuries, is often called 'Nestorian' although the word is now rejected by scholars and by the 'Church of the East' itself. Condemned at the Council of Ephesus in 431.

Nicene Creed   a popular name for the *Niceno-Constantinopolitan Creed.

Niceno-Constantinopolitan Creed   the revised Creed of Nicaea, probably produced at the Council of Constantinople in 381.

non-Chalcedonian one who disagrees with the Council of Chalcedon and especially with its famous 'definition of faith'.

Novatianism a schismatic tendency of the third-century Church that objected to liberal attitudes toward receiving back the lapsed into the Church. Novatian was a bishop of Rome and both he and his followers seem to have had orthodox doctrinal beliefs. Canon 8 of the Council of Nicaea addressed the problem of Novatianism.

orthodoxy from Greek *ortho*, 'right', and *doxa*, 'opinion' or 'belief'. Correct belief or doctrine, in contrast with '*heresy'.

patriarchate originally the residence of a patriarch or chief bishop; now the area over which he has authority. The word 'patriarch' (Greek *patriarches*), originally meaning 'ruler of a family', was used widely during the period of the councils with different shades of meaning. From the sixth century onwards it was used officially of the bishops of the five main patriarchates: Rome, Constantinople, Alexandria, Antioch and Jerusalem.

Paulianists followers of Paul of Samosata (third century). Paul taught a form of *adoptionism and *Dynamic Monarchianism. They claimed that God was ultimately a unity and that the Logos came upon Jesus during his lifetime. Canon 19 of the Council of Nicaea says that they must be rebaptized in order to be received back into the Church.

Pelagianism the teaching of Pelagius and others in the fifth century that human beings can attain their own salvation without the aid of divine grace. It was condemned in a canon of the Council of Ephesus in 431.

perichoresis from Greek *peri*, 'around', and *choreo*, 'to go on', 'come on' or 'make room for another'. A concept in the thought of the *Cappadocian Fathers and John of Damascus for the 'co-inherence' or 'relationality' of the members of the Trinity.

Photinians followers of Photinus (fourth century), who taught a version of *Sabellianism and also denied the pre-existence of Christ. Photinus was condemned at the Council of Constantinople in 381.

pneumatology from Greek *pneuma*, 'spirit', and *logos*, 'word'. Teaching about the Holy Spirit.

Pneumatomachoi Greek, 'Spirit fighters'. A group who denied the divinity of the Holy Spirit in the fourth century against the *Cappadocian Fathers. See also *Tropici.

pre-existent existing before the creation of the universe and of time.

procession (of the Holy Spirit) the ultimate status of the Holy Spirit in relation to the Father, and, according to Western theology, the Son.

proskunesis Greek, 'veneration' or 'honour', referring to the adoration given to the image of Christ and the saints in an icon. The term was used by John of Damascus and by the Second Council of Nicaea in 787 in contrast to *latreia* or worship, due to God alone.

Quartodecimans from Latin, 'fourteen'. Those who believed that Easter should be celebrated on the feast of the Jewish Passover itself, i.e. 14 Nisan.

Sabellianism the Modalistic *Monarchianism of Sabellius in the early third century.

schism a formal split in the Church.

Semi-Arians those Arians who thought that the Father and the Son were alike or similar rather than completely different.

Septuagint or LXX from Latin *septuaginta*, 'seventy' (hence 'LXX'). The ancient Greek translation of the Hebrew Bible. The tradition that it was translated by seventy translators who came up with identical texts can be found in the *Letter of Aristeas*.

Soteriology from Greek *soteria*, 'salvation', and *logos*, 'word'. The theology or doctrine of salvation.

Spirit fighters see *Pneumatomachoi, *Tropici.

subordinationism the doctrine that the Son is a lesser being than the Father.

synod a local council.

synousiasts from Greek *sun*, 'with', and *ousiai*, 'substances'. Followers of the teaching of Apollinarius who claimed that in Christ the divine and the human substances were united, resulting in a single substance. Like Apollinarius, they undermined the humanity of Christ.

Thalia Greek, 'banquet'. The songs of Arius by which he popularized his views. They survive only in fragments.

theopaschitism from Greek *theos*, 'God', and *pascho*, 'to suffer'. The claim that God the Son, or the Logos, suffered in Jesus when he died on the cross.

Theotokos from Greek *theos*, 'God', and *tokos*, 'bearer'. A title for the Virgin Mary. Nestorius' alleged rejection of this word brought it to the centre of christological concern in the fifth century. It was key to the dispute between Cyril and Nestorius and to the Council of Ephesus in 431.

traditor Latin, 'traitor', 'betrayer' or 'hander-over'. A Christian who had betrayed Christ and other Christians and who had lapsed in faith during Diocletian's persecution (303–12 CE), especially by giving up copies of Scripture. See also *lapsi.

trinitarian   concerning the Trinity or the concept of God as triune, that is, consisting of three persons: Father, Son and Holy Spirit.

Tropici   another name for the *Pneumatomachoi or *Spirit fighters of the fourth century. So called because of their 'tropological' or allegorical use of Scripture.

typology   the practice of using an Old Testament figure or event to shed light on a New Testament figure or event, as when Paul uses Adam or Abraham in order to illustrate his understanding of Christ.

via negativa   see *apophatic.

Bibliography and further reading

Books referred to below have been chosen because they are likely to be in university libraries or in bookshops. They are suggested only as possible starting places for further study.

Texts of the councils and related documents

Bettenson, Henry, and Maunder, Chris (eds) (1943/1999), *Documents of the Christian Church* (Oxford: Oxford University Press).
  A very useful collection of documents from two thousand years of Christian history, including many relevant to the councils.

Hardy, Edward R. (ed.) (1954), *Christology of the Later Fathers* (Philadelphia: Westminster Press).
  A collection of the writings of some of the key theologians of the period, along with other important documents.

L'Huillier, Peter (1996), *The Church of the Ancient Councils: The Disciplinary Work of the First Four Ecumenical Councils* (Crestwood, NY: St Vladimir's Seminary Press).
  Includes documents and discussions of the canons of the first four ecumenical councils, relating them to the Church today.

Stevenson, J. (ed.), revised by Frend, W. H. C. (1957/1987), *A New Eusebius: Documents Illustrating the History of the Church to AD 337* (London: SPCK).
  A substantial collection of important texts from the period indicated.

Stevenson, J. (ed.), revised by Frend, W. H. C. (1966/1989), *Creeds, Councils and Controversies: Documents Illustrating the History of the Church, AD 337–461* (London: SPCK).
  Likewise a substantial collection of important texts from the period indicated.

Tanner, Norman P. (ed.) (1990), *Decrees of the Ecumenical Councils*, 2 vols (Washington, DC: Georgetown University Press).
  Includes the texts of the decrees of the seven councils.

General works

Angold, Michael (2001), *Byzantium: The Bridge from Antiquity to the Middle Ages* (London: Phoenix).
  An informative account of the history of the Byzantine Empire, including the rise of the city of Constantinople and the iconoclasm controversy.

Davis, Leo Donald (1983), *The First Seven Ecumenical Councils (325–787): Their History and Theology* (Wilmington, DE.: Michael Glazier).
   A detailed historical account of the seven councils.

Ferguson, Everett (ed.) (1999), *Encyclopedia of Early Christianity*, 2nd edn (London and New York: Routledge).
   A very useful and detailed work covering many of the topics discussed in this book.

Hall, Stuart G. (2005), *Doctrine and Practice in the Early Church*, 2nd edn (London: SPCK).
   A detailed, scholarly introduction to the period up to and including Chalcedon. Covers liturgical practice as well as history and doctrine.

Houlden, Leslie (ed.) (2003), *Jesus: The Complete Guide* (London and New York: Continuum).
   A comprehensive encyclopaedia covering most of the issues discussed in this book.

Kelly, J. N. D. (1958/2003), *Early Christian Doctrines* (2003 edn London: Continuum).
   A detailed account of early Christian belief from a doctrinal standpoint.

McGuckin, John Anthony (2005), *The SCM Press A–Z of Patristic Theology* (London: SCM Press).
   A very useful dictionary covering all aspects of the seven councils, the people involved and the controversies concerned.

1 In the beginning: The titles of Jesus

Brown, Raymond E. (1994), *An Introduction to New Testament Christology* (New York: Paulist Press).
   A short introduction to some key themes and titles in New Testament Christology.

Dunn, James D. G. (2003), *Christology in the Making: An Inquiry into the Origins of the Doctrine of the Incarnation*, 3rd edn (London: SCM Press).
   A detailed scholarly discussion of the development of the idea of the incarnation, covering all the texts and titles discussed in the present book, and more.

Hurtado, Larry W. (2003), *Lord Jesus Christ: Devotion to Jesus in Earliest Christianity* (Grand Rapids, MI: Eerdmans).
   A comprehensive study of what early Christians up to the late second century believed about Jesus and how this played a part in their lives and worship.

2 A tale of two cities: Antioch and Alexandria

Barnes, Jonathan (2000), *Aristotle: A Very Short Introduction* (Oxford: Oxford University Press).
   A concise introduction to the philosophy of Aristotle.

Ehrman, Bart D. (2003), *Lost Christianities: The Battles for Scripture and the Faiths We Never Knew* (Oxford: Oxford University Press).
A detailed study of the many different forms of Christianity before the Council of Nicaea, focusing on the emergence of orthodoxy and heresy, and on Christian texts that did not make it into the New Testament canon.

Hare, R. M. (1982/1996), *Plato* (Oxford: Oxford University Press).
A concise introduction to the philosophy of Plato.

Russell, Norman (2006), *The Doctrine of Deification in the Greek Patristic Tradition* (Oxford: Oxford University Press).
A thorough study of the idea of *theosis* or 'divinization' in some of the key theologians of the period.

Trigg, Joseph W. (1998), *Origen* (London: Routledge).
A collection of some of the key writings of Origen, with a useful introduction.

3 There was when he was not: The Council of Nicaea (325 CE)

Anatolios, Khaled (2004), *Athanasius* (London: Routledge).
A useful collection of some of Athanasius' works, with a solid introduction.

Pohlsander, Hans A. (1996), *The Emperor Constantine* (London: Routledge).
A very short introduction to the life and reign of Constantine the Great.

Rubenstein, Richard E. (1999), *When Jesus Became God: The Struggle to Define Christianity During the Last Days of Rome* (London: Harcourt).
A popular account by a Jewish author of the Arian crisis, the rise of Emperor Constantine and the Council of Nicaea.

Williams, Rowan (2002), *Arius: Heresy and Tradition*, 2nd edn (London: SCM Press).
A very detailed scholarly study of the theology and significance of Arius, portraying him as a conservative thinker rather than as an innovator.

4 Of a rational soul and a body: The Council of Constantinople (381 CE)

Basil the Great (1980), *On the Holy Spirit*, tr. David Anderson (Crestwood, NY: St Vladimir's Seminary Press).
An English translation of Basil's own work on the Holy Spirit, with an introduction.

Meredith, Anthony (2000), *The Cappadocians* (Crestwood, NY: St Vladimir's Seminary Press).
A short, lively introduction to the three Cappadocian Fathers, covering their lives and times, and their theologies.

Rousseau, Philip (1994), *Basil of Caesarea* (Los Angeles: University of California Press).
A comprehensive biography of Basil, covering his life and theology.

5 Holy Mary, Mother of God? The Council of Ephesus (431 CE)

Koester, Helmut (ed.) (1995), *Ephesos, Metropolis of Asia: An Interdisciplinary Approach to its Archaeology, Religion, and Culture* (Valley Forge, PA: Trinity Press International).
   A collection of essays on a wide variety of aspects of the history, archaeology and religion of ancient Ephesus.

Pelikan, Jaroslav (1996), *Mary Through the Centuries: Her Place in the History of Culture* (New Haven and London: Yale University Press).
   A popular look at the ways in which Jews, Christians and Muslims have portrayed Mary.

Russell, Norman (2000), *Cyril of Alexandria* (London: Routledge).
   A useful collection of Cyril's key works, with an introduction.

Wessel, Susan (2006), *Cyril of Alexandria and the Nestorian Controversy: The Making of a Saint and of a Heretic* (Oxford: Oxford University Press).
   A detailed historical and theological study of the controversy between Cyril and Nestorius.

6 Truly divine and truly human: The Council of Chalcedon (451 CE)

Brox, Norbert (1994), *A History of the Early Church* (London: SCM Press).
   A short history of the Church up to and including the Council of Chalcedon.

Sarkissian, Karekin (1965), *The Council of Chalcedon and the Armenian Church* (New York: The Armenian Church Prelacy).
   The Council of Chalcedon and its Christology from an Armenian perspective.

Sellers, R. V. (1953), *The Council of Chalcedon: A Historical and Doctrinal Survey* (London: SPCK).
   A detailed scholarly account of the Council of Chalcedon, covering historical and doctrinal issues.

7 Natures, energies and wills: Two councils of Constantinople (553 and 680–1 CE)

Allen, Pauline, and Hayward, C. T. R. (2004), *Severus of Antioch* (London: Routledge).
   A collection of some of the main works of Severus, with an introduction.

Louth, Andrew (1996), *Maximus the Confessor* (London: Routledge).
   A collection of some of the key writings of Maximus, with an introduction.

Meyendorff, John (1997), *Christ in Eastern Christian Thought* (Crestwood, NY: St Vladimir's Seminary Press).
   A study of the development of Christology from the fifth century to the iconoclasm controversy, written from an Eastern Orthodox perspective.

8 Icons and idols: The Second Council of Nicaea (787 CE)

Baggley, John (1988), *Doors of Perception: Icons and their Spiritual Significance* (Crestwood, NY: St Vladimir's Seminary Press).

A short, lively introduction to icons, covering important aspects of history and spirituality.

John of Damascus (1980), *On the Divine Images: Three Apologies Against Those Who Attack the Divine Images*, tr. David Anderson (Crestwood, NY: St Vladimir's Seminary Press).

John of Damascus' own text on icons, translated into English with a useful introduction.

Ouspensky, Leonid (1978, 1992), *Theology of the Icon*, 2 vols (Crestwood, NY: St Vladimir's Seminary Press).

Volume 1 is a thorough study of the issues surrounding icons from their beginnings to the Second Council of Nicaea in 787. Volume 2 takes the story up to the twentieth century.

Pelikan, Jaroslav (1974), *The Christian Tradition: A History of the Development of Doctrine*, vol. 2: *The Spirit of Eastern Christendom (600–1700)* (Chicago: University of Chicago Press), ch. 3.

A solid introduction to the theology of icons during the centuries of iconoclasm.

Theodore the Studite (1981), *On the Holy Icons*, tr. Catherine P. Roth (Crestwood, NY: St Vladimir's Seminary Press).

Theodore's own text on icons, translated into English with a useful introduction.

9 The councils today: Positions and prospects

Binns, John (2002), *An Introduction to the Christian Orthodox Churches* (Cambridge: Cambridge University Press).

An informative discussion of the various Orthodox churches from the time of Constantine to the present day.

Chaillot, Christine, and Belopopsky, Alexander (1998), *Towards Unity: The Theological Dialogue Between the Orthodox Church and the Oriental Orthodox Churches* (Geneva: Inter-Orthodox Dialogue).

A collection of some of the main agreed statements made between various members of the Orthodox and other churches.

Gregorios, Paulos, *et al.* (1981), *Does Chalcedon Divide or Unite? Towards Convergence in Orthodox Christology* (Geneva: World Council of Churches).

A collection of agreed statements and essays, focusing on issues that have traditionally separated the Chalcedonian and Non-Chalcedonian churches.

Ware, Timothy (1993), *The Orthodox Church*, 2nd edn (London: Penguin).

A solid, general introduction to the Orthodox Church, covering history, faith and worship.

Website

Internet Medieval Sourcebook, home page
<www.fordham.edu/halsall/sbook.html>.
  This website includes the full texts of an enormous number of works relevant
to this study.

Index

177